Around the Table

"Around the Table is a richly engaging exploration of the Eucharist, as experienced by the first people to 'taste and see'—the disciples and saints who knew Christ best. Imagine gathering around the table of the Lord with the likes of Paul, Mary Magdalene, Cleopas, and Mary. This is a feast like no other and R. Scott Hurd makes us all welcome at the banquet. Take and read—you'll be glad you did. It's a terrific book and Scott Hurd has hit one out of the park!"

Deacon Greg Kandra
Catholic blogger and journalist at *Aleteia*

"R. Scott Hurd's passionate appreciation for the Eucharist has given rise to this wonderful book exploring the many meanings of the sacrament. *Around the Table* is a profound treasure trove of ancient wisdom, theological reflection, and personal spiritual engagement that causes one to think in new ways about the mystery of the Eucharist and awakens a driving enthusiasm to know more."

Sr. Donna Markham, O.P.
President and CEO of Catholic Charities, USA

"As twenty-first-century Christians, we find it difficult, if not impossible, to re-enter the world of the gospels. With wisdom, insight, and great tenderness, R. Scott Hurd has given us a way. I highly recommend this book for anyone seeking a more experiential understanding of the Eucharist."

Paula Huston
Author of *Simplifying the Soul*

Around the Table

the Table

Retelling the Story of the Eucharist through
the Eyes of Jesus' First Followers

R. SCOTT HURD

AVE MARIA PRESS AVE Notre Dame, Indiana

© 2016 by R. Scott Hurd

Founded in 1865, Ave Maria Press is a ministry of the United States
Province of Holy Cross.

www.avemariapress.com

Paperback: ISBN-13 978-1-59471-655-3

E-book: ISBN-13 978-1-59471-656-0

Cover image © RMN-Grand Palais/Art Resource, NY.

Cover and text design by Katherine Robinson.

Printed and bound in the United States of America.

Library of Congress Cataloging-in-Publication Data is available.

To Diane

You held compassion for me when I could not.

You held my hand after it had long been empty.

You took hold of my heart and lifted it to yours.

Pax et Bonum et Benedictum, always.

contents

· ·

preface

The Eucharist has been compared to a multi-faceted gem that reveals different elements of beauty when it is held to a light and slowly turned in one's fingers. While this image might be a bit cliché, it has certainly rung true for me. For most of my conscious life, I have actively participated in, taught about, and been fascinated by this sacrament. The Eucharistic celebration has been a weekly constant in my life since I was a boy, and during certain graced periods, I've had the opportunity to participate daily. As I reflect on my personal experiences of the Eucharist, I recall moments of transcendence, words that warmed my heart, and messages that cut to my core. I've known the consolation of being united with a community of believers that spans the globe and embraces people of every age, culture, and language and forms a body bound together by one greater than ourselves. Gathered around the Eucharistic table, I have been conscious of entering a reality not confined by time and space and through which I have been healed, strengthened, renewed, and challenged to become the person our loving God created me to be.

The Eucharist is a mystery because its true reality is understood only by faith. Faith, however, seeks understanding, and my fascination with the Eucharist led me to learn more about this gift in order to more fully appreciate its richness. What began as self-study was later enriched by formal study, which in turn led to opportunities to share my knowledge with children and adults, in classrooms and with family, online and from the pulpit. And now, finally, I have written a book that I hope will lead those who read it to cherish the Eucharist along with me.

Early on in writing this text, I found that my manner of presenting its content took an unexpected turn. Initially, I had intended to write a series of chapters on different aspects of the Eucharist with the experience of a biblical figure serving as a springboard. However, the experiences of the biblical figures soon dominated the narrative, despite the fact that scripture provided little information about these individuals. I turned to modern scholarship, archaeological research, ancient traditions and stories, and my own imagination to fill in the personal details of these people. I looked beyond what the biblical record, history, or even the sometimes fantastic legends about these figures might provide for us. I fully engaged my imagination and seasoned it with the traditions of the Church.

St. Ignatius of Loyola, the sixteenth century founder of the Jesuits, gave me license to use my imagination this way. In his famous *Spiritual Exercises*, Ignatius proposed a way of praying in which we place ourselves in a scene from the life of Jesus—smelling the scents, hearing the sounds, perhaps seeing through another's eyes, imagining how we might respond if we had been there in person. Interestingly, I had never before prayed in this fashion before writing this book, but I'm delighted that it came rather easily to me. Yet that shouldn't have come as a complete surprise; after all, the imagination is a gift from God, and we can certainly use it to better understand God's other gifts, such as the Eucharist.

In presenting the Eucharist through the eyes of Jesus' family, friends, and followers—through the eyes of saints—I'm hoping that readers might come to appreciate saints in a new way. It's tempting to view saints as otherworldly, remote, and exotic. Classical art can depict them as sanitized; popular art can make them appear comic. However, in life, they were real, flesh-and-blood men and women with strengths and weaknesses, hopes and dreams, triumphs and failures. While they were certainly heroic, they were not perfect. I've sought to convey these realities throughout the book not only so that saints can be appreciated for who they really were but also so that readers might, in them, see something of themselves.

Like us, saints were also creatures of their own ages and cultures, living at particular points in history. I have tried to reflect this in my imaginative presentations of the experiences and recollections of those saints who were Jesus' contemporaries. For instance, they employ language about the Eucharist that was common for the first generation of Christians and avoid titles and terms that didn't emerge until later. That's why they typically refer to the Eucharist as the "breaking of the bread" and "the Lord's Supper" rather than "sacrament," "the Mass," or even "Eucharist." Nor do they refer to anyone as "priest," as they would likely have used instead a Greek word, *presbyter*, which applied to whom we today would identify as "priest" or "bishop."

With the passage of time, a rich treasury of traditions and stories has arisen around many saints, especially several featured in this book. Some of these traditions and stories are likely nothing more than pious legends; they aren't always grounded in historical facts, and some are, quite frankly, unbelievable to modern ears. However, we can value them as important elements of Catholic culture and self-understanding, reflections of the deep faith of earlier generations. I have alluded to some of these traditions and stories in a number of chapters not only to honor our heritage but also because they can instruct and help us understand the faith our ancestors have handed down to us—a faith which includes a deep reverence for the Eucharist.

Of course, it is the scriptures and not ancient legends that are indispensable when seeking to understand the

Eucharist. Scripture is filled with Eucharistic references and intimations. Many readers will likely be familiar with what might be called the "foundational" scripture passages about the Eucharist: the Last Supper narratives, the "bread of life" discourse in the sixth chapter of John's gospel, and the accounts of the multiplication of loaves and fishes. Details about these events sometimes differ between the four gospels, and I have mixed and matched elements of these different portraits of Jesus throughout the book. Many other Eucharistic references in scripture are less well known, however, especially those in the Old Testament, written before the time of Jesus. These came to be understood as having Eucharistic significance only through spiritual reflection over the course of time. I've sought to incorporate allusions to many of these passages so that readers might come to a fuller appreciation of both scripture and the Eucharist.

A fuller appreciation of the Eucharist is, of course, the primary objective of this work. In an imaginative way, I have chosen to highlight different facets of this gem that it might be cherished in its fullness: a sacred meal and sacrifice which offers forgiveness and healing, binds us together as one, fills us with God's own life, offers a foretaste of heaven, empowers us to serve and evangelize, commits us to caring for the poor and fighting injustice, shapes our understanding of work, expresses our gratitude and thanksgiving to God, and allows Jesus to be present in our midst. My own appreciation of these realities has certainly deepened through writing this book, and it is my hope that this will also be the experience of those who read it.

INTRODUCTION

Imagine living two thousand years ago in what today we call the Holy Land. A woolen tunic is fastened at your waist; palm bark sandals are on your feet. You find yourself standing on a grassy hillside, one person among a large gathering of men, women, and children. It's springtime, it's warm, and sunlight sparkles on the Sea of Galilee behind you. You feel a gentle wind—a faint echo of the violent gale that blew through last night. Because of the breeze and surrounding crowd, you strain to hear the words of a distant figure who lately has been causing quite a sensation. People have been buzzing about who he might be, given the miracles he's performed, the way he's gotten under the skin of the religious authorities, and his inspiring teaching, which is delivered with a power and authority never before seen. Some think he is one of the prophets of old, delivering a new message from God. Others wonder if he might be John the Baptist, risen from the dead after being beheaded by Herod, the local tyrant. Many are prepared to whisk him away and proclaim him king. A few dare to whisper that he might even be the promised Messiah. His name is Jesus.

The day before, you and thousands of others spent the afternoon listening to Jesus speak. Most of those with you were poor, and they had not brought food with them. As the day wore on, many began to think that perhaps it was time to return home. Stomachs were growling, attentions wandered, and a long walk back lay ahead. But then Jesus did something astounding: he took a handful of loaves and fishes from a little boy, blessed them, and told his band of disciples to pass them out. Somehow, to everyone's amazement, there was more than enough for everyone to eat, and baskets were filled with leftovers. People were full, happy, grateful, and dumbfounded. They shouted with joy and praise, and some burst into song. It's no wonder that after Jesus and his friends left that evening, many in the crowd walked all night, trying to find them again. Including you.

Jesus was eventually sighted on the other side of the Sea of Galilee. And just as yesterday, you and all the rest now hang on his every word. He speaks of the loaves and fishes with which he fed everyone the day before, as they are still very much on people's minds. Given that stomachs are growling again, a second serving would be gladly welcomed. But then Jesus begins to speak of other food: a bread that never perishes; a bread that, if you eat of it, will allow you to live forever. Now everyone is really paying attention, as they've never heard anything like this before. A number of people cry out and beg Jesus for some of this bread. Others nod their heads in agreement. Excited whispers run through the crowd, until Jesus says something that stuns everyone into silence, making their jaws drop: that he himself is that bread of which he speaks and that bread is his "flesh." What's more, he insists that if anyone wishes to truly live, not only do they need to eat his "flesh," they must also drink his "blood."

Upon hearing this, many around you begin to murmur and complain. Some are shocked, others are confused, and quite a few are flat-out horrified. The Jews in the crowd know that they are forbidden to drink blood. Blood is essential to life, and since all life belongs to God, to drink it is sacrilege. And then there is the business of eating flesh. What on earth? What else could that be but cannibalism? A good number shake their heads in disgust. "This saying is hard!" they complain. "Who can accept it?" They shrug their shoulders and walk away, disappointed that the inspiring miracle worker has turned out to be a madman. He'd filled their bellies, but they cannot stomach what he has to say.

The thought of joining them crosses your mind, but something holds you back. As you watch them walk away, you turn to Jesus, wondering what he'll do next. Will he run after those who have left, shouting at them to wait so he can explain what he really means? Not at all. Instead, after letting the crowds go, he faces and questions his close friends—the same ones who had passed out the bread and fish the day before. Do they also wish to leave, Jesus asks? Is his latest teaching just too much to take? One of them, a fisherman named Peter, speaks on their behalf. You hope he might say, "Lord, we understand completely what you're talking about. Eating your flesh and drinking your blood makes perfect sense! We get it! There's no need for you to explain." But he does nothing of the sort. Instead, he, too, like those who left, throws up his hands in frustration. "Where shall we go?" he wonders out loud. "You have the words of everlasting life." As you understand him, what Peter says to Jesus is this: "Even though we want to believe that what you're saying is true, we have no idea what you're talking about."

Peter and his companions are just as puzzled as anyone else about what Jesus said that day. Nevertheless, they have faith in him. He has certainly surprised them many times before, and this incident is simply another in a string of teachings and miracles that have left them scratching their heads. But for them, there is no turning back. They are too committed, even though at times they have felt overwhelmed and confused. They know that Jesus loves them deeply, in spite of getting frustrated with them now and then. They love him, too, as best they can, in spite of their hang-ups and fears. So they continue to follow him. And because they do, they will eventually come to understand what he means by eating his "flesh" and drinking his "blood," even though it will take them awhile.

They will gain added insight a year from now, in Jerusalem, while gathered in an upper room of a friend's home. Along with tens of thousands of other pilgrims, they will journey to Jerusalem for Passover to remember how God freed their ancestors from slavery in Egypt. They will go there to celebrate the Passover meal as they have done year after year with their families since childhood. The rituals, the prayers—they are all comfortingly familiar. One always knows what comes next; there are no surprises. Except for that night. They will expect Jesus to say the traditional words they know by heart. But once again, Jesus will do something shocking. After he blesses and breaks the bread before him, he will say that it is his "body" and give it to them to eat. Then he will take his cup of wine, call it his "blood," and pass it around for everyone to drink.

Even before this, the disciples' minds will be racing that evening. They will recall that just days before, Jesus was welcomed into the city by a joyful, excited crowd. Nevertheless, he repeatedly insisted that he would soon be betrayed and killed. Fear and confusion will have gripped their hearts. Yet in spite of their feelings, they will surely recall that day by the sea when Jesus first spoke of his body and blood. When they eat the bread Jesus gave them and drink from his cup, they will likely have an "Aha!" moment and think, "So this is what he was speaking about!" They will understand a bit more than they had before. But there will still be so much they don't understand; there will be so many things yet to learn. Jesus will know that, and he'll say so. "I have much to tell you," he will confess, "but you cannot bear it now." They will indeed be able to bear it later. After Jesus has risen from the dead and ascended into heaven, their understanding of what Jesus meant that day about his "flesh" and "blood" will continue to grow. They've always had faith. But their faith sought understanding. And so, with the guidance of the Holy Spirit, they will come to ever-deepening insights about what Jesus said and did.

Like the disciples, we, too, have faith. We believe Jesus, but sometimes the things he said can leave us puzzled. That can be especially true of the Eucharist, the sacrament Jesus gave to us that one Passover night, surrounded by his disciples in that upper room. The Eucharist is a great gift and a priceless treasure, but it is also, at its heart, a mystery. A "sacred mystery," as the Church has come to call it. And mysteries, by their very nature, can sometimes be hard to comprehend. That's why we speak of things being "shrouded" in mystery. In the mystery of the Eucharist, we're invited to take it on faith that ordinary bread and wine become the body and blood of Jesus. At times, this may seem difficult to swallow. However, through our faith which seeks understanding, we can chew over this mystery in our minds, and it can become much more digestible.

In seeking to understand the Eucharist, we can find help from Jesus' friends, family, and followers—those who had a front-row seat to what Jesus said and did. As first-hand witnesses, they enjoyed a privileged perspective from which to appreciate the richness of the Eucharist. Since their time, the Church's understanding of that richness has grown, and we are beneficiaries of that development. However, in order to grasp where we've gotten to today, it's helpful to start at the beginning—with those who lived, prayed, and journeyed with Jesus. To see through their eyes, we can use our imaginations, just as we did at the beginning of this chapter. Using imagination to pray and understand our faith is a time-tested and saint-sanctioned practice in our Catholic tradition. It's not about making stuff up in our heads. Instead, it's about using one God-given gift—the imagination—to appreciate another God-given gift—the Eucharist.

Through imagination, we can join the apostles at that final Passover meal, what we today call the Last Supper. With the Bible as our guide, we can join them on other occasions, too: at the foot of Jesus' cross, outside his empty tomb, on the dusty road to Emmaus, at Jesus' feet as he proclaimed the Good News. There isn't an event in Jesus' life that we cannot share, thanks to imagination. However, Jesus did many more things than were recalled in the Bible. The Bible itself says that. And that's even more true for those who lived alongside Jesus. In the Bible, some were simply mentioned by name; they were part of the group but weren't singled out from the crowd. But the crowd remembered them. Stories were told, and in some cases, legends were created. All of this tradition has been passed down to us. It has helped us understand who these people were and why we honor them with reverence and devotion. It can also feed our imaginations and help us appreciate the treasure of the Eucharist.

In each chapter of this book, we will take the place of a specific friend, follower, or family member of Jesus in order to consider a particular aspect of the Eucharist and hopefully grow in gratitude for this gift. We live some twenty centuries later, and we weren't fortunate enough to have been eyewitnesses to all Jesus said and did. In a sense, we stand on their shoulders. Yet that doesn't prevent us from also standing in their sandals, seeing through their eyes, coming to know what they knew, and growing to love what they loved.

Questions
for Journaling, Contemplation, or Conversation

1) What elements of the Eucharist do you find confusing or mysterious?

2) Does imagination play a role in your life of faith? In what ways?

Stop and Pray

Bread of Life,
My faith in you seeks understanding.
Help me use the gift of imagination to better understand
the gift and mystery of the Eucharist, that I might be healed,
strengthened, consoled, and united with you and my brothers and sisters.
Help me become the saint you call me to be.
Amen.

Going Deeper

John 6:1–15	Jesus Feeds Hungry Crowd with Loaves and Fishes
John 6:16–21	Strong Winds on the Sea of Galilee
John 6:22–59	The Necessity of Eating Jesus' Flesh and Blood
John 6:60–69	Reactions to Jesus' Teaching
Mark 14:12–26	Jesus Observes Passover with His Disciples
Mark 11:1–11	Joyful Crowds Greet Jesus Upon Entering Jerusalem
Mark 9:30–32	Jesus Predicts His Betrayal and Death
John 16:12–15	Jesus Explains that His Disciples Have Much to Learn

1. CLEOPAS

FOOD FOR
THE JOURNEY

Who was St. Cleopas?

"Were not our hearts burning within us?" asked St. Cleopas of his companion after listening to a mysterious stranger who accompanied them from Jerusalem to Emmaus on the day of Jesus' resurrection. At the end of that journey, the stranger was revealed as Jesus himself when he blessed, broke, and shared bread in Cleopas's Emmaus home. Before this encounter, Cleopas may have been one of seventy disciples Jesus had called to prepare towns for his upcoming visits, and it is said that he was ultimately martyred for his faith in the very house where he had hosted the risen Jesus. Tradition tells us that he was the older brother of Joseph, the husband of Jesus' mother, Mary, and that it may have been his own wife, also named Mary, who was his traveling partner on that first Easter.

• • • • • •

The road is packed with travelers this day. With few exceptions, they are all heading in the same direction: away from Jerusalem and toward home, wherever that may be. A good number are prepared for long journeys

1

to far-distant destinations. They travel in caravans of oxen-pulled carts laden with provisions and passengers. Some ride donkeys while others walk. The cloaks they wear become blankets at night as they sleep on the ground in the open air. You, too, travel by foot. But you don't have far to go—only seven miles, as a matter of fact. Normally, this trip takes you just a few hours. Today, however, it seems to last an eternity as you shuffle with slumped shoulders, a head hung low, and a heart filled with grief.

As tradition requires, you had remained in Jerusalem for the entire feast of Passover: seven whole days. Friends had allowed you to stay with them, as it was next to impossible to find a room at a boarding house. Visitors from every corner of the world had so packed the city that it swelled to more than four times its normal size. Most came by land, but some arrived by ship. Like you, the vast majority were Jews, pilgrims come to celebrate the memory of the Exodus, when the Lord had freed your ancestors from slavery in Egypt. But there were others, too: merchants, thieves, curiosity seekers, and Roman soldiers on high alert for the slightest whiff of trouble.

You had been to Jerusalem for Passover many times before. After all, it wasn't that far away, and it had always been a joy to go. You loved the Lord and were happy to celebrate the wonders he had done for your people. You also enjoyed the sights and sounds of the city. The Temple ceremonies inspired wonder and awe, and the hustle and bustle of the crowds was exciting, even if the presence of Roman soldiers added an element of tension. When the festival ended and it was time to return to your village of Emmaus, you were usually sorry to leave, in spite of your exhaustion and eagerness to attend to duties back home.

This year, however, you are glad to put Jerusalem behind you. While on the road, you turn and gaze at the city you have loved, numb with shock and bewilderment. The sky is beautifully clear and blue, but you hardly take notice. It doesn't seem to matter. Just days before, that sky filled with billowing smoke as priests burned the organs and entrails of thousands of slaughtered Passover lambs at the great Temple's high altar. One of those lambs had been yours. It had been perfect, without blemish, just as God had commanded. You and your companions had brought it to the Temple in the morning. A member of your party slit its throat, while a priest collected the blood in a bowl and then sprinkled it at the base of the altar where coals were burning. The lamb was hung on a hook, and the inedible parts were removed and placed on the altar. Finally, you left with the remainder of the animal to roast for the evening meal.

You ate it, of course, just as scripture and the ancient traditions commanded. But the festive air that normally accompanied this meal was missing, as the previous several days had been filled with danger. When you had first entered the city, you had followed behind Jesus of Nazareth, who you were convinced would be a great leader of the Jews. He was riding a donkey, as was proper for a king approaching a city in peace. Great crowds were shouting, waving palm branches and casting their cloaks before him, while Roman soldiers anxiously surveyed the scene and fingered their swords. And they weren't the only ones who were nervous. Certain Jewish leaders were enraged at this spectacle. "Teacher, rebuke your disciples!" they demanded. Others simply scowled with folded arms as they whispered sideways comments to their companions. On a few faces, you thought you glimpsed fear.

Tensions mounted in the days that followed, especially after Jesus caused a disturbance in the Temple by overturning moneychangers' tables and driving out the merchants with a whip. He was furious, and that in turn made his adversaries even angrier. They tried to trip him up at every opportunity by tricking him into saying the wrong thing. Jesus was too clever, however. His wisdom shamed his opponents into silence and even won him some grudging respect. Nevertheless, they were undeterred and continued to plot to kill him. And since Jesus was a target, his followers would become targets, too. Jesus himself had acknowledged as much. "You will be hated by all," he had warned, "because of my name."

Gloom hung over your Passover meal like a pall. You went through the motions, doing what you were supposed to do, but it was all perfunctory. What should have been a celebration of liberation had been robbed of its joy. The wine you drank only added to your depression. Neither you nor your companions had any idea where Jesus and his apostles were that night. For all you knew, they might not even be in the city. You hoped that Jesus was safe, but you sensed that he was likely in trouble. After all, hadn't he insisted that he would be killed while in Jerusalem? You were scared for him. And you were scared for yourself.

The following morning, your worst fears were confirmed. Jesus had been arrested overnight and brought to the headquarters of Pilate, the Roman governor, to stand trial. While watching the proceedings from afar, trying to stay inconspicuous at the edge of the spectators, you wondered how it had all come to this. Until this moment, you had been convinced that Jesus was a mighty prophet, sent from God to save his people—your people. He had even chosen you and sixty-nine others to prepare towns for his coming by announcing the arrival of God's kingdom. You had done this with enthusiasm, and in gratitude, Jesus had promised that your name was written in heaven. But now there he was, a bloodied, beaten prisoner, standing in mute silence while the crowds jeered, demanding his death. Why did he endure this? He had healed the sick, walked on water, even brought the dead back to life! How, then, could he allow himself to die? But that's precisely what he did. When he was taken away to be crucified, you couldn't follow to watch. Feeling faint, you collapsed against the nearest wall, buried your face in your hands, and wept.

This memory now preoccupies your thoughts as Jerusalem fades from view. Because you move so slowly, you stay by the side of the road, letting others pass as the sounds of clopping hooves, creaking wheels, and chirping cicadas fill the air. Sheep bleat, donkeys bray, and camels grunt and groan while you and your companion speak. Other conversations waft by, punctuated by children's laughter and snippets of song. But then there is another voice—a stranger's voice that is oddly familiar—and it is directed at you: "What are you discussing as you walk along?"

At first, his words bring you to a standstill, as the answer is almost too painful to give. But then you become indignant, wondering out loud how on earth this individual could not know all that has been taking place. The stranger, however, is unruffled. It seems that he knows everything that has happened. Even more, he claims to know why it has happened, and he seems disappointed that you and your friend do not. "Was it not necessary," he jibed, "that the Messiah should suffer these things?" You don't answer, partly from embarrassment but mostly because you want him to continue talking—which he does, for quite some time, speaking of the scriptures and holding you spellbound. It feels as if your heart is on fire.

Your pace, once so slow, has quickened, and you are now standing erect, so as to be more attentive to the stranger's piercing, captivating words. All too soon you arrive at Emmaus. Is the stranger going to continue on? Will he not stay? It is almost nightfall, after all. It is normal, even expected, for you to offer him hospitality. But when you ask him to stay, you are being more than polite; you want to hear more of his teaching. Your despair has begun to crack, chipped away by his words of hope.

Sharing a meal, however, is the first order of business. The three of you gather around a small table in the middle of the room. You and your companion recline on mats on the earthen floor, but the stranger sits upright. Taking bread in his hands and raising his eyes to heaven, he offers a prayer of thanksgiving. *"Barukh ata Adonai Eloheinu,"* he intones in Hebrew. "Blessed are you, Lord our God, King of the Universe." You had expected him to say this. But you do not expect what happens next. When he breaks the bread, offers you half, and looks into your eyes, you suddenly understand who has joined you along the way. It is Jesus himself, somehow no longer dead but very much alive. Yet as soon as you recognize your guest, he vanishes from your sight.

Wasting no time, you rush back to Jerusalem. It is dark, but the moon is almost full and the road nearly empty. What had been a slog just hours before now becomes somewhat of a race. When you reach the city, breathless and elated, you head straight to the house of John Mark, where that very morning you had bid farewell to those who were closest to Jesus. His mother, Mary, is there, of course; you also know her as the wife of your little brother, Joseph. And as you quickly survey the upper room where they are gathered, you also see the rest of the disciples—all except Judas. They are as excited to see you as you are to see them. When you begin to speak of what has happened, you are interrupted, as your friends share amazing news of their own: Jesus has risen from the dead and appeared to Simon Peter! Never mind that angels had announced this resurrection to women in your group early that morning. Everyone now believes, and they hang on your every word as you tell how Jesus walked with you on the way and made himself known in the breaking of the bread.

Your tiny home will never be the same, graced as it has been with the presence of Jesus. You will think of that day often, especially on the Sabbath when you gather for the Lord's Supper with your fellow believers, who address each other as "brother" and "sister." Outsiders will label you "Nazarenes," a disparaging reference to Jesus' hometown. New converts in distant places like Antioch will call themselves "Christians." But your community will refer to itself as "The Way" because following Jesus has become your way of life. You like that name. It suggests a journey and will remind you of your own unforgettable journey when the Lord walked beside you, taught you, and fed you with bread through which he revealed his very self.

One day, it will become clear to you: the life of faith is itself a journey, and as on any journey, you need to be fed and nourished or else you aren't going to get very far. As a disciple, Jesus called you to walk on his Way. He didn't, however, leave you to travel alone. He accompanies you and even supplies the provisions: words that set your heart aflame and a meal that strengthens your spirit. Fortified with these gifts, you will know that there will be no turning back as you make your way to your destination.

The destination, of course, is to be with Jesus for all eternity. And as providence will have it, your portal to that destination will be the very room in which you entertained the Lord, for it will be there that you will die a martyr for your faith. This time, however, Jesus won't vanish. You will no longer be on the Way, for broken bread will have led to a heavenly banquet.

Questions
for Journaling, Contemplation, or Conversation

1) Who or what has sustained you along life's journey?

2) When have you been touched by God? How did you recognize God's presence?

Stop and Pray

Dear Lord,
At times I travel life's path with joy and confidence.
At other times I'm weary and discouraged
and wonder if I'm on the right path.
Please journey at my side
and sustain me with the Bread of Life
as I make my way home to you.
Amen.

Going Deeper

Luke 24:13–35	Cleopas on the Road to Emmaus
Exodus 12:1–11	Instructions for Sacrificing Passover Lambs
Luke 19:28–40	Jesus' Entry into Jerusalem
Matthew 21:12–17	Jesus Cleanses the Jerusalem Temple
Matthew 22:15–22	Jesus' Adversaries Try to Trick Him
Luke 21:17	Jesus Warns His Disciples of Hatred
Luke 18:31–34	Jesus Predicts His Passion
Luke 23:1–25	Jesus' Trial Before Pilate
Luke 10:1, 17–20	Jesus Appoints the Seventy [-two]

Early Titles for Jesus' Followers:

Acts 24:5	*Nazarenes*
Acts 11:26	*Christians*
Acts 9:2; 19:9, 23; 22:4, 14, 22	*Followers of "The Way"*

2. PAUL

BODY OF CHRIST

Who was St. Paul?

St. Paul, formerly Saul of Tarsus, either wrote or directly inspired at least thirteen of the twenty-seven books of the New Testament. His powerful letters and extensive travels to spread the Gospel were first inspired by a miraculous encounter on the road to Damascus with the risen Jesus, who demanded "Saul, Saul, why are you persecuting me?" As a Roman citizen and convert from Judaism, Paul was an unlikely yet a most effective missionary to the Gentiles. Paul's writings, which predate the gospels, helped Christians understand their unity with Jesus, both through the celebration of the Eucharist and his presentation of the Church as the body of Christ. His final journey took him to Rome, where he was martyred around the year AD 67.

• • • • • •

You are a man on a mission. As a Hebrew, you are one of God's chosen people. That alone is something to be proud of, maybe even to boast about. But you are no ordinary Hebrew. You are one of the elite, with impeccable credentials, a noble lineage, and a top-tier education. You are self-confident and self-righteous, too. In Hebrew

11

circles, you are known as Saul; with everyone else, you introduce yourself as Paul.

Above all else, you are zealous for your religion. Every law and tradition is precious to you, and you follow them to the letter. As you understand it, not only is your faith something to be practiced, it is also something to be protected. It has certainly been threatened from the outside, especially by the Romans who govern your homeland, which you believe God gave your people. They tolerate your religion, for now, but they have also imported their own gods and rituals. Tensions simmer under society's surface. You often hear talk of revolution, and sometimes violence breaks out. You, however, are a Roman citizen, and in your eyes, Roman rule is not the greatest threat. The larger threat comes not from the outside but from the inside: namely, those crazy, misguided fools who claim to follow Jesus of Nazareth, who was crucified just a few short years ago.

You had heard people speak of him while he was alive—quite a bit, actually. There were excited reports of healings and miracles, and he allegedly had a gift for teaching as well. At the time, you dismissed all this as silly talk. Yet, unlike with others who had come before him, even Jesus' death hasn't put an end to things. His fanatical followers insist that he has risen from the dead and are spreading this nonsense everywhere. Even worse, people are embracing it, and the little sect he started continues to grow. It has gone from being a nuisance to a significant problem. Resurrection isn't the issue; you believe in that. But this fellow was a quack, a charlatan, a heretic. He hailed from Nazareth, of all places. Nevertheless, this Jesus' legacy seems to be catching on with more and more people. Some say it is spreading like wildfire. But to your eyes, it is growing like a cancer. People should know better. They should listen to the experts who really know what they're talking about. Experts like you.

And so you are determined to destroy this movement before its tentacles can reach even further. Armed with a special mandate from the Jewish authorities in Jerusalem to defend the faith, you've became notorious among the Nazarenes, as Jesus' followers are sneeringly called; they shake with terror at the mere mention of your name. With this reputation and your marching orders in hand, you head north to the city of Damascus, where you will arrest the Nazarenes who worship there. Your intention is to bring them back to Jerusalem for interrogation and maybe even execution. That will be a test of how loyal they are to this Jesus.

Along the way, you meet many people on the dusty road: merchants and soldiers, pilgrims and thieves, drifters and diplomats. The last person you expect to meet is Jesus himself. He is dead, after all. Or so you think. But then, while riding on horseback, it happens. A blindingly bright light envelops you. Stunned, you fall out of your saddle to the ground, where you cower in shock and fear. Then a voice speaks, powerful and commanding, yet compassionate at the same time. You can't see the speaker, but he knows exactly who you are. "Saul, Saul," the voice insists, "why are you persecuting me?"

"Who are you, sir?" you ask with trembling voice, even though you can guess as to who is now addressing you. The voice confirms your suspicions: "I am Jesus, whom you are persecuting."

From that moment on, your life takes a 180-degree turn. You continue to Damascus, not to persecute Jesus' followers but to join them. One of their number, Ananias, welcomes you to the community. You need him, not just for his introduction but also because you were struck blind at your encounter with Jesus. To restore your vision, Ananias lays his hands upon you and prays. Something like scales fall from your eyes, and you can see again. But thanks to that healing, you realize thatyou have been blind in other ways, too. To have persecuted these good people was wrong, and you have also been wrong about Jesus himself. Soon you begin to preach fearlessly about Jesus, just as you had formerly preached against him. This complete about-face is welcomed by some, but it creates enemies of others who once considered you an ally. They try to stop you. The former hunter becomes the hunted, and you have to flee for your life in the middle of the night.

Under the cover of darkness, you seek the safety and solitude of the Arabian Desert. You stay there for some time—more than two years, as a matter of fact. It is a fruitful period of renewal and conversion. You think and pray. The words of the Hebrew prophets you know by heart take on new meaning as you come to see that they point to Jesus. And the words of Jesus himself, the very ones he spoke to you, take on new meaning as well. "Why do you persecute *me*?" he had asked.

You now wonder, *Why did he say "me"?* You'd never met him before; you'd thought he was dead. How on earth could you persecute him? Why didn't he say "my people" or "those I love" or something like that? That would have made much more sense.

But then it dawns on you: Jesus and his followers are one; to speak of one is to speak of the other. It isn't simply that they are bound together by a common purpose or form a tightly knit unit out of faith or fear or love or whatever. Instead, Jesus and his followers are like a body—a human body, to be precise. Just as a human body is one while made up of many parts, so Jesus and his followers are one body with many members. This "body of Christ," however, isn't held together with skin, bones, and tissue. Instead, the bond is the Holy Spirit, whom you yourself received when you were baptized by Ananias, the same day you regained your sight.

Jesus had a physical body, of course. That came with being human. Jesus' body enabled him to speak, get around, and touch others so he could heal their wounded bodies and, more importantly, their wounded souls. But having a body had its limitations, too. It restricted Jesus in time and space; he couldn't be in two places at once (at least before his resurrection). Even though he had travelled extensively, only a fraction of the people in a small corner of the world had gotten a chance to see and hear him in person. After all, his ministry lasted just three years.

Then again, it didn't. You have seen his ministry continue through his followers—the members of his body. This body is able to do what Jesus' physical body had allowed him to do: to preach, to touch, to travel, to suffer. Jesus acts through his body when its members act in his name. Yet this body does more than just continue Jesus' ministry. Instead, it extends and expands it to where Jesus himself hadn't had the opportunity to go. Jesus' followers, you now realize, don't simply represent Jesus. Instead, in a very real sense, they *are* Jesus. That's why Jesus could say to you on the road to Damascus, "Why are you persecuting *me*?" In truth, to persecute his followers was to persecute him. They are one.

Yet there is another insight you gain in that desert. It comes to you while you are fasting. In your hunger, you sometimes fantasize that the stones scattered around you might actually be bread. Some are round and brown, and in the noonday sun, you can see the heat rising from them. If you squint just right, they look like freshly-baked loaves, still hot from the oven. At times, it almost seems as if you can smell their aroma. You recall that, while in Damascus, you had heard how Jesus, when he fasted in the desert, had been tempted to actually change stones into bread. Performing such a miracle isn't possible for you, of course. But when your stomach growls, and your head feels faint, sometimes you wish it was.

On one occasion when your thoughts turn to bread, a Sabbath meal you had shared with Ananias and his friends comes to mind. You had joined them for the Lord's Supper, as they called it—something they did every week. It was a joyful celebration, and everyone seemed thankful. Scriptures were read, prayers were offered, and gifts were brought to distribute to the poor. It reminded you of the Passover meals you had observed every year for as long as you could remember. Yet it was different, too, especially when Ananias took bread, broke it, and spoke words Jesus himself had spoken: "This is my body, which will be given for you." At first hearing, you had thought this shocking, even scandalous. It went against your training, your traditions. Yet at the same time, you knew it to be true.

And now, in the desert, it all becomes increasingly clear. Jesus had, and still has, a body. His followers, bonded in the Spirit, are also his body. And the bread that is broken at the Lord's Supper is his body, too. All three are connected; one cannot be rightly understood without the others. You conclude that those who are one with Jesus are fed with Jesus in order to become more like Jesus; by eating the bread which is Jesus' body, one more fully becomes who one already is. This process is essential, actually. After all, how else could ordinary men and women love as Jesus loves? How might they forgive as he forgives? How can they persevere as he persevered and come to see the world as he sees it? Not by *imitation* but by *incorporation*—by being a part of his body and being nourished by that body. The goal of following Jesus, you've come to understand, is not just to be *like* Jesus but to *be* Jesus. As you will one day write, "I live, no longer I, but Christ lives in me."

This truth will become very precious to you. Later, you will travel the world, taking Jesus to places where he himself had been unable to go: Asia, Greece, Cyprus, Malta, Spain, and the great city of Rome. Everywhere you go, you will teach about Jesus' body, and you yourself will preside at the meal in which bread becomes that body. At times, you will see it misunderstood and misused, leaving you frustrated and angry. The Christians in the city of Corinth will concern you the most. "The bread that we break," you will ask them in frustration, "is it not a participation in the body of Christ?" This was such a vitally important point that you will use harsh words to take some of them to task: "For anyone who eats and drinks without discerning the body, eats and drinks judgment on himself."

You will be tough like that when you need to be. But then again, you have always been a pretty tough character. Time and again, you will endure torture or injury. You will be whipped and beaten, stoned and left for dead, and even shipwrecked at sea—three times! Your body will be abused and broken, and you will bear the scars to prove it. You will suffer greatly in your body, just as Jesus suffered in his, and this knowledge will give you courage and comfort. And because you are a member of his body, you won't simply suffer *like* Jesus; you will suffer *with* Jesus. Your wounds will be his wounds, and his wounds will be yours. "I bear on my body," you will write to friends, "the marks of Jesus." Your wounds will testify to your faith as his wounds testified to his love.

Suffering, however, won't be the end of the story—neither his nor yours. Jesus died in his body, rose in his body, and ascended to heaven in his body. For the members of his body, who feed on his body, that is their hope as well. "For as often as you eat this bread," you will insist, "you proclaim the death of the Lord until he comes." And when he comes, you continue, Jesus "will change our lowly body to conform with his glorious body," and his friends, those who were "one bread, one body," will then be united with their "one Lord" in an eternal chorus of praise.

Questions
for Journaling, Contemplation, or Conversation

1) What experiences have you had that significantly changed the course of your life? Think and pray about what they have meant to you.

2) In your life of faith, has it ever seemed as if you were part of something bigger than yourself? Why or why not?

Stop and Pray

Lord Jesus,
By your Holy Spirit I am joined to fellow Christians
and to you in your Body, the Church.
Through the gift of the Eucharist,
nourish me with your body and blood.
May I extend your ministry of love,
and more fully become who I already am.
Amen.

Going Deeper

Philippians 3:4–6	Paul's Hebrew Credentials
Galatians 1:11–16	Paul's Zeal for the Jewish Law
Acts 22:28	Paul's Roman Citizenship
Acts 23:8	Pharisees' Belief in Resurrection
Galatians 1:13–14	Christians Persecuted by Paul
Acts 9:1–2	Paul's Mandate to Arrest Christians
Acts 9:3–5	Jesus Appears to Paul on the Road to Damascus
Acts 9:6–19	Ananias and Paul

Acts 9:19–22	Paul Begins to Preach
Galatians 1:16–17	Paul in Arabia
Matthew 4:1–3	Jesus Tempted to Change Stones into Bread
1 Corinthians 11:20	Eucharist Called the "Lord's Supper"
1 Corinthians 10:16–17; 11:28–29	Bread of the Eucharist is the Body of Christ
Galatians 2:20	Christ Lives in Paul
Acts 13–21; 27–28	Paul's Extensive Travels
2 Corinthians 11:23–27	Hardships Experienced by Paul
Galatians 6:17	Paul Bears the Marks of Jesus
1 Corinthians 11:26	Jesus' Death Proclaimed by the Lord's Supper
Philippians 3:21	Bodies Glorified at Jesus' Return
Romans 16:25–27	A Body as a Model of the Church
1 Corinthians 10:16–17; 12:12–27	
Galatians 3:26–28	
Ephesians 1:22–23; 2:11–22; 3:3–9	
Colossians 1:24–27	

3. Bartholomew

Foretaste of Heaven

Who was St. Bartholomew?

St. Bartholomew is listed as an apostle in the gospels of Matthew, Mark, and Luke. However, tradition identifies him as one and the same with Nathanael, who is encountered only in the fourth gospel. Nathanael was a native of Cana in Galilee, and at one time may have been a follower of John the Baptist. He was introduced to Jesus through the encouragement of Philip, who invited him to "come and see." Initially, Nathanael was skeptical, but when Jesus revealed that he had seen Nathanael under a fig tree before Philip had approached him, Nathanael was astounded and proclaimed Jesus to be the "Son of God." He then became a disciple along with Philip. After the ascension of Jesus, Bartholomew/ Nathanael is said to have taken the Gospel to Armenia, where he was martyred.

• • • • • •

John Mark's home has become part headquarters, part sanctuary, and part refuge. The first time you were here, just several weeks ago, it had been in secret. You and the other apostles had been with Jesus in the upper room, celebrating the Passover meal. The day after Jesus was crucified, you had all gathered here again to grieve,

21

process your shock, and for those who had run away, attempt to unburden your shame. It was a safe house, and at that time, only Jesus' inmost circle knew where it was. Three days later, you were still there. The door was tightly bolted as a precaution. Nevertheless, to everyone's astonishment, the risen Jesus appeared in your midst, wished everyone peace, and replaced your fear with joy. During the next forty days, Jesus spent time with your group, encouraging, healing, and speaking about the kingdom of God. Finally, just before he ascended to heaven, Jesus instructed all of you to remain in Jerusalem and wait for the coming of the Holy Spirit, which you did, for nine whole days—usually together, and often in John Mark's upper room.

There has been so much to discuss there. After all, God's promises have been fulfilled! Jesus is indeed the Messiah for whom everyone had hoped, even if he wasn't quite whom they'd expected. He'd been dead but now is alive! He had taught you much, but many questions still remain unanswered. What will happen next? And just what, or who, is this "Holy Spirit" Jesus promised was coming? When you aren't praying, you debate these matters late into the night, as it is hard to sleep given all the excitement. Peter often speaks about being "fishers of men." Your old friend Philip recalls the day when Jesus fed a huge crowd with just a handful of bread and a pair of fish. Your mind, however, keeps going back to Jesus' ascension, when a cloud raised him to heaven and left you speechless atop the Mount of Olives, staring at the sky, your eyes wide with astonishment.

Thoughts of the Ascension recall for you an earlier time—the very day you had first met Jesus, in fact. It was a lovely afternoon, and you were resting in the shade under a favorite fig tree. From that beautiful hilltop spot, you could see Galilee stretch before you for miles. In the valley below were farmlands lush with flax, wheat, and barley, rich vineyards, olive groves, and endless rows of trees ripe with dates, pomegranates, and more figs. Behind you was your home village of Cana. It was a humble place, but you loved your town and were proud of it. Everyone in Cana was like family, really. Most of you actually *were* family. You were especially fond of a young, engaged couple; the whole town was looking forward to their wedding, which would probably last for days. Your neighbors liked you, as well; they knew you to be honest and devout, a solid citizen with a ready smile and an impish sense of humor.

They also knew you to be something of a thinker, even a dreamer. Under that fig tree was your favorite spot to reflect. A brown patch of worn earth at the foot of its twisting roots marked where you'd sit, enjoying respite from the heat, gazing at the clouds, and listening to the leaves rustle in the breeze. It was quiet there and peaceful. Sometimes you'd lie back with your hands behind your head, fall asleep, and dream. But more often than not, you'd simply daydream. You'd consider all kinds of things, such as what you would have for dinner that night. Would you bring home figs from your tree? Most likely. Yet you would contemplate grander subjects as well: God, his laws, the meaning of life, and questions such as *"What happens when I die?"*

For most of the people you knew, the answer to that question was simple: when you died, your spirit, or "shade," would descend to Sheol, the dreary abode of the dead. That was standard Jewish belief, and you didn't care for it very much, truth be told. Everyone would go there: righteous and unrighteous, rich and poor, young and old, men and women, master and slave. Sheol wasn't necessarily a place of punishment, but it wasn't a reward, either. It certainly wasn't much of an existence as the shades were thought to dwell in dust, darkness, and silence. You'd heard the old story of how the disgraced King Saul, disguised and in secret, had the

witch of Endor conjure up the shade of the prophet Sam-
uel, who was none too pleased to have been roused from
his sleep. Sleep, in fact, seemed to be the best description
of what the shades in Sheol actually did. No wonder that
it was sometimes likened to a pit with swallowing jaws,
from which no one would return. The prospect of Sheol
terrified you, frankly. If that was the final destination
of all human existence then death was no friend. It was
something to be feared.

Others had drawn that same conclusion and thrown
up their hands in despair. If everyone dies and shares a
similar fate, what's the point of living a good life? Why
not just eat, drink, and be merry? Yes, God might be
kind and merciful. But to what end? After all, rain falls
on both the just and the unjust. Bad things happen to
good people, and good things happen to bad people.
The rich get richer, and the poor get poorer. It didn't
seem fair at all. Perhaps this was simply a mystery too
big for mere mortals to ponder. Nevertheless, thoughts
like this troubled many. They certainly troubled you
when you let your thoughts wander under the fig tree.

Then again, there were some who thought and
spoke of other possibilities: possibilities that expressed
a hope for something better than the endless sleep of
Sheol. You had heard how prophets from past ages had
foretold of new heavens and a new earth, where hunger
and sickness would be no more and every tear would
be wiped away. Peace and justice would reign, and the
lion would lie down with the lamb. Sorrow and sadness
would make way for happiness and joy, and hearts of
flesh would replace hearts of stone. Weapons of war
would be destroyed, as would even death itself. Those
whom death had once claimed would live again; the
shades in Sheol would rise from the dust. Not just in
spirit but in body, too. Dry bones would reassemble, be
covered in flesh, and receive the breath of life.

Resurrection of the dead, it was called—especially by the Pharisees, the "separated ones." Everyone knew who they were. Pharisees were devout, disciplined, and learned; they could always be picked out of the crowd by the long blue tassels at the ends of their cloaks. Some Pharisees—those who were convinced that they were more righteous than everyone else—left you feeling uncomfortable and inferior. Yet there were some Pharisees you liked, especially the ones who would answer your questions. You enjoyed a good debate, and they typically did, too. In particular, you appreciated some of the things they had to say, such as when they spoke of resurrection. Their words filled you with peace and hope and seemed to fit with your understanding of the God you prayed to under the fig tree.

Philip would sometimes join you under the tree. He wasn't from Cana, hailing instead from Bethsaida, where he was a fisherman. Both of you were Jews from Galilee; that was a bond you had in common. Yet you had another tie that bound you together even more closely: your love of the Lord and your search for the truth. At one time, Philip had been a follower of John the Baptist, and he had once convinced you to hear him speak. John the Baptist's message of repentance had cut you to the heart, and you and Philip discussed it for hours on end. You had come to expect this sort of thing from your friend.

The last thing you ever expected, however, was for Philip, breathless from running and beside himself with excitement, to announce that he had just met the Messiah—the one about whom Moses and the prophets had written. Better yet, Philip had continued, the Messiah was in Galilee. Normally, you would have trusted his judgment, but this report left you feeling deeply skeptical. Your skepticism only grew when you found out where he was from: nearby Nazareth, of all places—an unimportant, undistinguished, impoverished backwater.

"Can anything good come from Nazareth?" you joked out loud. You meant it as a light-hearted dig at a neighboring village, but still, the Messiah would certainly not come from there. However, you didn't wish to disappoint your friend, so you reluctantly left the shade and comfort of your fig tree to follow Philip and meet his messiah from Nazareth: Jesus, the son of Joseph.

After walking for some time, Philip spotted Jesus speaking to a small group by the side of the road. As you approached him together, Philip was exuberant, but you felt cautious and cynical. You caught Jesus' eye, however. With a smile on his face, he made his way toward you and announced, "Here is a true Israelite. There is no duplicity in him." It was a good-natured compliment, and you liked him at once. While still skeptical that this Jesus was who Philip claimed he was, you sensed that somehow he knew you, and you said so out loud. Jesus laughed. "Before Philip called you," he explained, "I saw you under the fig tree."

You froze in your tracks, trying to process his words. Thoughts spun in your head: *How does he know me? How could he have seen me if we've never met before? And under my fig tree, no less!* Then it dawned on you: Philip was right; Jesus must be the Messiah. From Nazareth. Standing right in front of you and smiling. Almost impulsively, you blurted out: "Rabbi, you are the Son of God!" Jesus laughed again and made a promise that you would never forget: "You will see the sky opened and the angels of God ascending and descending on the Son of Man."

These words immediately sounded familiar; you had heard them somewhere before. Then you remembered. It was at the synagogue, on the Sabbath. The rabbi had unrolled the scroll of scripture and read a story about Jacob, one of the great patriarchs of your people. One night in the wilderness, he had a dream while he slept with his head on a rock—an arrangement you recall thinking sounded terribly uncomfortable. But while on that rock, Jacob dreamt of angels ascending and descending on a ladder to heaven at the very spot where he rested. When he awoke, he concluded that he was standing at the gate of heaven. He named the place *Beth-el*, which means "House of God."

From that day you'd first met him, Jesus' promise would often come to mind. You'd wonder: *Will I see what Jacob himself had dreamed of? When will it happen? Have I missed it somehow?* For some time, you reflected on this, eager with anticipation but puzzled at the same time. One afternoon, however, you received what you were sure was a key to answering your questions. Jesus was speaking to a large crowd who, just the day before, he had miraculously fed with a small handful of loaves and fishes. They wanted more, but Jesus explained that there was an even greater food they should hunger for: a bread that comes down from heaven and gives life to the world. People began to cry out for this food until Jesus stunned them by insisting that he himself was that bread—a "living bread"—who had come down from heaven. To ensure that they understood, he repeated this two more times. By then, many had heard enough because what they'd heard they couldn't accept. They left. But you didn't because you were convinced that Jesus was the Messiah. And besides, you wanted to hear more.

You would hear much more, especially that first time you sat in John Mark's upper room, celebrating Passover with Jesus. That evening, Jesus prayed and taught at length. He commanded everyone to love one another and then announced that he would soon go away. This news distressed you and your friends, but Jesus spoke words of comfort. While he would be going to his Father's house, he would later return so all who loved him could dwell there, too. "I will go back again and take you to myself," he said, "that where I

am you also may be." This promise, which you now
knew described more than any earthly journey Jesus
would take, filled you with hope for a future life far
more appealing than the gloom of Sheol. You could now
anticipate not an existence of dwelling in dust, darkness,
and silence but in the very house of God.

After that evening, you understood that Jesus had
not only come down from heaven; he would also go back
up. His promise to you, made three years before, now
began to make much more sense. In spite of your fear
and your grief, you somehow clung to this truth as a lifeline the following day as Jesus hung dying on a hilltop.
And it remained with you three days later when Jesus,
risen from the dead, appeared to you in John Mark's
upper room. It was no ghost who stood before you that
day; it was truly Jesus himself, in the flesh. Your hopes
of resurrection, shaped by those past friendly debates
with Pharisees, had now been realized. However, you
still awaited the fulfillment of Jesus' promise to you.

That would happen weeks later outside the village
of Bethany, atop the Mount of Olives, just a few miles
from Jerusalem. As you gathered around him, Jesus told
you and your companions to wait in Jerusalem for the
Holy Spirit to come. Then, to your complete astonishment, Jesus was lifted into the sky on a cloud, and two
men in white appeared at your side, as if from nowhere.
Immediately you recognized them as angels—the very
angels Jesus had predicted you would see on that fateful
and life-changing afternoon that began under your fig
tree. When the angels insisted that Jesus would return
in the same way he had just left, you rejoiced in that
promise. And you rejoiced that Jesus' personal promise
to you had finally been fulfilled.

Now, back in Jerusalem, in the upper room, you
reflect on all these things. Jesus had indeed come down
from heaven and has since returned there to prepare a
home for you. Yet what about the meantime? Is Jesus

completely absent? Has he departed simply to leave you and the other disciples to your own devices? No; the gift of the Holy Spirit you will soon receive will make that abundantly clear. The Spirit will bring to your mind Jacob's dream, in which he saw the angels ascending and descending at Bethel. For Jacob that night, heaven and earth had met at a *place*. You now realize that heaven and earth met in a *person*. That person is now in heaven, but he can still be met on earth in the "bread of heaven," which Jesus said was his own flesh and which will give a little taste of the resurrection life. "Whoever eats this bread," he assured you, "will live forever." A life far better than the endless gloom of Sheol. And one which, through that bread, you could begin to enjoy even now.

Questions
for Journaling, Contemplation, or Conversation

1) What do you think about life after death?

2) When or where have you experienced or glimpsed heaven on earth?

Stop and Pray

O Son of God,
Thank you for offering the Church a taste of heaven
in your Bread of Life.
Sustain me in the hope that you will come
and take me to yourself,
where peace and justice reign,
and sorrow gives way to joy.
Amen.

Going Deeper

John 20:19	The Risen Jesus Appears to His Disciples
Acts 1:3–5	Jesus Instructs Disciples to Await the Holy Spirit
Acts 1:9–12	Jesus Ascends into Heaven
John 21:2	Nathaniel from Cana in Galilee
John 2:1–11	Wedding at Cana
Psalm 88 Isaiah 5:14; 14:11; 38:10–11 Job 10:21–22; 17:13–16 Ecclesiastes 9:1–10	Descriptions of Sheol
1 Samuel 28:3–5	Saul and the Witch of Endor
Job and Ecclesiastes	Old Testament Reflections on "Why Live a Good Life?"
Isaiah 2:4; 25:6–8; 65:17–25 Ezekiel 36:26–28; 37:1–14	Anticipation of a New Heaven and Earth
John 1:43–51	Nathanael Introduced to Jesus
Genesis 28:10–17	Jacob's Dream at Beth-El
John 6:22–68	Jesus Teaches That He Gives "Living Bread"
John 13:31–14:6	Disciples Promised Rooms in the Father's House
John 20:19–23	Appearance of the Risen Jesus
Acts 1:6–12	Ascension of Jesus into Heaven

4. Longinus

Initiation

Who was St. Longinus?

According to tradition, St. Longinus was a centurion of the Roman army and a native of Italy. He commanded the detail of soldiers who carried out Jesus' crucifixion and is said to have been the one who thrust a lance into Jesus' side. As blood and water poured forth, Longinus exclaimed, "Truly, this was the Son of God," and was healed of a blindness inflicted by an old battle wound. Following this experience, Longinus left the army, was baptized by the apostles, and took his new faith to Cappadocia, in modern-day Turkey. A statue of Longinus may be found at the crossing of St. Peter's Basilica in Rome, and what is claimed to be a part of his lance is in one of the four pillars over the altar.

• • • • • •

This crucifixion has been planned for quite some time. Crucifixions are expensive and require advance preparation; they can't simply happen on the spur of the moment. The wood needed for crosses is scarce in this part of the world and must be secured beforehand. Also, soldiers are essential at crucifixions to prevent riots from breaking out or friends of the condemned from trying to save them. Today, your company is scheduled for crucifixion duty. As a Roman centurion, you are their commanding officer. When you first received your orders, you had been informed that two criminals would be put to death. At the very last minute, a third condemned man has been added to the roster: a certain Jesus from Nazareth, whose name you've heard often over the past several days.

Whenever you are on crucifixion duty, you have to ensure that the soldiers under you stay alert and on guard. This is especially important in Jerusalem, where your company currently serves. Jerusalem is such a dangerous city that you and your fellow soldiers are housed in a massive fortress, the Antonia, lodged against the city's defending wall. However, it isn't forces outside the city that pose the constantly imminent threat: it is the Jewish fanatics who live within. They hate you and anything and anyone else associated with the Roman Empire. Fair enough, you have concluded; you have come to hate the Jews.

While growing up, you had known some Jews but not very well; they largely kept to themselves. Their traditions and religion are quite different from yours, yet that hadn't bothered you very much. The Jews in Jerusalem bother you a great deal, however, just as much as your presence in their city seems to bother them. Since your arrival, you have learned that Jerusalem is their holy city and that they believe their god himself dwells in the big temple at the city's heart, atop a hill. In your travels with the army, you have seen many impressive temples to different gods. This one isn't too bad, you think, but it certainly isn't the finest you have encountered. But to these Jews, it is the center of their world. It is so sacred to them that, even though they are under Roman rule, there remains an understanding that no one who isn't a Jew can enter interior parts of the building. If the Roman army were to force the issue, there would surely be a violent backlash.

Then again, there always seems to be threat of a riot. This last week has been especially tense. Tens of thousands of Jews arrived in Jerusalem for a religious festival: "Passover," they call it. You don't understand what it is all about, and you don't really care, but given all the visitors and their intense religious fervor, the entire Roman army in Jerusalem has been on high alert. Pilate, your governor, even brought in reinforcements from surrounding regions. Normally, Pilate doesn't live in Jerusalem. He detests the Jews, and they feel the same way about him. The acrimony is mutual. But he remains here this week to stamp out any signs of trouble.

Jerusalem and the surrounding region of Judea was Pilate's first diplomatic post. It was given to him not because of his talent or experience but because he is rich, ambitious, and well-connected. He is also extraordinarily cruel. You will never forget how he once ordered the slaughter of Jews in Jerusalem who had gathered near their temple to protest. They had heard rumors that Pilate intended to steal from their temple treasury to build a new aqueduct, and they were furious. But Pilate had no patience for such challenges to his power. His instructions were that you and other soldiers were to mingle within the crowd, hidden under civilian cloaks, and wait for a signal to draw your swords and attack the Jewish protesters. You and your companions followed orders; by the end of that day, scores of people, including many innocent bystanders, were left dead or dying in the streets.

Since that time, opposition to Pilate has intensified, which places you and all Romans in Jerusalem in even greater danger than before. Many Jews, especially those who live outside the big towns and cities, refuse to pay their taxes. Certain of them band into groups which try, little by little, to chip away at Roman power through acts of violence. They have become a threat not just in the countryside but in the city as well. Some are called

"Zealots." Others are known as the *sicarii*—the "dagger men"—who infiltrate a crowd and stab their targets—either Romans or Roman sympathizers—and then vanish from sight. They terrify the locals. They frighten you, too.

On the morning of the scheduled crucifixions, you carefully watch the crowd that has gathered for any sign of threatening activity from the dagger men or anyone else. Although you are an experienced soldier, surveying the scene is particularly difficult for you: you are blind in one eye from a battle wound received years before. Thankfully, a good number of soldiers flank the crowd in the courtyard of the Antonia to witness the trial of Jesus, who was evidently arrested the night before. The popular interest in Jesus' fate is deeply troubling, and tensions are high. Just days before, this crowd had welcomed Jesus into Jerusalem with great fanfare. You had actually watched Jesus ride past you on the back of a donkey. The atmosphere was frenzied, and you frequently fingered the hilt of your sword. But as for Jesus himself, he didn't appear to be much of a threat at all.

This morning is the first time you've seen Jesus since that day, and he seems even less of a threat to you now than he did then. You can see that he's been beaten, but he holds himself with great courage and dignity. What a contrast to Pilate, you think, who stands next to Jesus atop a high staircase. There he is, the chief local representative of the most powerful empire on earth, looking frightened and unsure, especially when the crowds insist, over and over again, that Jesus be crucified. Above all else, Pilate wants to avoid unnecessary trouble because he'll likely lose his job if matters get out of hand. He also has no real choice but to concede to the crowd's demands, as Jesus has been accused of claiming to be a king. Anyone proclaiming himself to be a king is a threat to Roman rule and therefore a rebel.

And the only suitable punishment for a rebel is death by crucifixion.

After Jesus is sentenced and whipped, he has to carry through the city streets the crossbeam of what will become his cross; he must bear it all the way to the crucifixion site of Golgotha, the "place of the skull," so called because caves in the site's hillside bear an eerie resemblance to the eyes and nose of a human skull. It is a fitting name for a gruesome place to which you and a handful of other soldiers march alongside Jesus. For him to carry the crossbeam is hard enough, as it weighs at least seventy-five pounds. But the whipping he has endured at the hands of a skilled torturer has managed to strip the skin off his back while keeping his muscles intact. Jesus is in excruciating pain as he struggles to make headway with his burden. He falls three times, weakened and exhausted, until finally, you force a bystander to help.

Normally, the suffering of a Jewish condemned criminal would not elicit any sympathy from you at all. Yet Jesus is different. He seems innocent; even Pilate himself, during the trial, admitted that he could find no guilt in him. But where were his supporters now? What had happened to the throngs that had welcomed him days before? The only people who give him any sympathetic notice today are a handful of weeping women. Then it dawns on you: those who had been excited about his arrival had been itching for a fight; they were looking for a champion to lead them in battle against the likes of you. But when Jesus failed to meet their expectations, they in turn failed to follow. You recall that some soldiers under your command had mocked Jesus, spat upon him, and slapped him in the face. At the time, you couldn't have cared less. But you begin to care now. Pity has replaced your contempt.

When you arrive at Golgotha, your detail of soldiers—*immunues*, or crucifixion specialists—set to work.

There are four of you altogether. As a sign that you are
the centurion in command, you carry your sword on
your left, and you keep your hand on your hilt to show
any potential troublemakers that you mean business.
You watch your men remove Jesus' clothes, bind his
arms to the crossbeam with cords, and drive six-inch
nails through his wrists. They then lift the crossbeam,
with Jesus hanging upon it, and affix it to a post in the
ground. Following this, there is nothing else to do but
wait. From your experience, sometimes crucifixion kills
a person fairly quickly; at other times it can take several
hours or even days. But you know that Jesus will be
dead by sundown, even if one of your men has to hasten
his death. After all, those are your orders.

These days, crucifixions don't normally have an
effect on you. As a soldier, you are acquainted with
death and have been trained to kill. Any compassion you
may have once felt vanished long ago. Until Jesus. As
he hangs dying, he doesn't curse, threaten, or plead for
mercy, even as he is taunted and jeered at by bystanders
and passersby. There is pain in his eyes but no hatred.
He says little, and he never speaks to you directly. But to
your shock, he prays for you and your soldiers. "Father,"
he gasps as he looks toward heaven, "forgive them; they
know not what they do." He has prayed to his god that
you would be pardoned for killing him! This god isn't
your god, but from that moment on, you want him to
be. In your heart, you become convinced that Jesus is
an innocent man. And when he finally dies with a loud
cry, as the ground shakes under a darkened sky, you
understand that he was more than just a man. "Truly,"
you exclaim aloud, "this man was the Son of God."

Your initial contempt for Jesus had become sympathy, which is now replaced by admiration and awe.
As you gaze up at Jesus, your soldiers break the legs
of the two men crucified alongside him to hasten their
deaths. But since Jesus does not appear to be breathing,

you yourself lance his heart, in case there is the slightest trace of life in him. It is a tiny act of mercy to conclude an immense act of cruelty. Unexpectedly, not only does blood pour forth but also water. It showers down upon you, soaking your head, shoulders, and torso. You have been covered with blood many times before. It had disgusted you, and you were always quick to wash it off. This time, however, you feel as if you have already been washed. Made clean, somehow. To your astonishment, the sight in your blind eye is completely restored. And to your joy, you feel as if your soul has been healed. You have just helped to kill this man. Yet, strangely and wonderfully, you yourself feel more alive than ever; almost as if you have been born anew.

As evening falls, friends of Jesus approach Pilate for permission to bury his body. After confirming with you that Jesus is indeed dead, Pilate consents. Jesus' body is laid in a rock tomb and sealed by an immense stone while you return to the Antonia, amazed by your restored vision and still feeling elated—although, excepting your healed eye, you aren't entirely sure why.

You will feel that way again, after Jesus' resurrection, and that time you will know why because Jesus' followers, of whom you will be one, will explain it to you. On that day, one of Jesus' disciples will plunge you into muddy waters. Yet, when you rise up, you will feel pure and cleansed—just as you did when you were soaked with blood and water at the foot of Jesus' cross. Your new friends will call this washing "baptism" and speak of it as the way to die with Jesus and be raised up to a new life in God's Holy Spirit. That evening, as it will be the first day of the week, you will take part in their sacred meal, the Lord's Supper. One of Jesus' disciples, who will be leading the prayers, will break bread and give some to you, declaring that it is Jesus' "body." Following this, you will sip from a cup of wine that, the same disciple will say, has become Jesus' "blood."

Your being washed with water and having received Jesus' body and blood will bring back the vivid memory of lancing Jesus' body and being showered with blood and water, and you will realize, in that moment of insight, the connection between baptism and the Lord's Supper. You alone had stood at the foot of the cross and been filled with joy and awe as you were soaked from Jesus' pierced heart. At the time, you had felt strangely renewed and restored; you had even felt that you had received the forgiveness for which Jesus begged his Father in his dying words.

In time, you will know that, through baptism and the Lord's Supper, everyone can stand at the foot of the cross as you had and then die and rise with Jesus to share a new life in the Holy Spirit: a grace-filled life of hope and faith. This life will begin at baptism, when one is truly born anew, and it will be nourished at the Lord's Supper by feeding upon, as Jesus himself had called it, the "bread of life."

As you will come to see, everyone who lives that life will undergo changes, as old ways are replaced by new. For you, it will mean laying down your weapons, taking off the armor of a Roman centurion, and putting on what some will call the "armor of God" by living a life not of violence and hatred but of peacemaking and love.

Questions
for Journaling, Contemplation, or Conversation

1) In what ways has God met your expectations? Exceeded them? Failed them?

2) Has your faith commitment led you to make significant life changes? If so, what kinds of changes have you made?

Stop and Pray

....

Christ Jesus,
Thank you for the new life of grace I received
in the healing waters of Baptism.
As I seek to nourish that life through the Eucharist,
please renew me in joy
and continue to restore my vision,
that I may always acknowledge you as truly the Son
of God.
Amen.

Going Deeper

....

John 12:12–16	Jesus' Entry into Jerusalem
John 18:28–19:16	Pilate's Trial of Jesus
John 19:17	Jesus Carries His Cross
Luke 23:27–29	Women Weep for Jesus
Matthew 27:27–31	Soldiers Mock Jesus
Matthew 27:45–54	Crucifixion of Jesus
Luke 23:34	Jesus Asks the Father to Forgive Soldiers Who Crucify Him
Luke 23:47	Centurion Proclaims Jesus' Innocence
Matthew 27:54	Centurion Proclaims Jesus to Be the Son of God
John 19:31–37	Blood and Water Pour from Jesus' Side
John 19:38–42	The Burial of Jesus
John 3:1–15 Romans 6:3–4	Baptism and Being Born Anew

5. mary

love

Who was Mary, the Mother of Jesus?

As was customary for the Jewish culture of her time, Mary was possibly as young as thirteen when she was betrothed to Joseph, her intended husband, and conceived her son, Jesus, through the Holy Spirit. She was a native of Nazareth, a small town in Galilee where she and Joseph raised Jesus. According to tradition and as implied by scripture, Joseph died before Jesus began his public ministry. Mary's strenuous days would likely have included drawing water, baking bread in a community oven, tending animals, preparing meals, and weaving cloth for her family's clothing. Her life was marked by trials and hardships caused by merciless rulers, unjust judges, and the persecution of Jesus, beside whom she stayed during his crucifixion. As Jesus is both her son and the Son of God, Mary is honored as the Mother of God.

• • • • • •

It is time to flee town. You are expecting and beginning to show. Although you are engaged to Joseph, you aren't married yet, and if people learn that you are pregnant, tongues will wag and fingers point. Neighbors and strangers alike will scorn you as a tramp, and your entire family will be publicly shamed. Some might insist that you be stoned to death; others will expect Joseph to end your engagement so he won't have to claim another's child as his own. If that happens, you might well be left homeless and penniless, consigned to a lifetime of hardship.

Both you and Joseph know how your child was conceived. It happened early one morning when you were visited by Gabriel, an angel. His appearing startled you, but Gabriel calmed your fears and announced that you were favored by God himself. Because of this, you would conceive through being overshadowed by something, or someone, called the "Holy Spirit." With humility, you embraced this news, and when Gabriel departed, you felt confused but elated. You were also, however, pregnant and unmarried.

When you told Joseph about it, he had been deeply distressed. He had wanted to trust you, but he struggled to accept that your child was conceived in anything other than the normal way, which meant with a man other than him. Who could blame him? He was angry, but mostly he felt sad; his spirit had been crushed. He loved you and had been counting the days until your wedding. Everything was ruined, he feared, until he, too, received a visit from an angel. Joseph's angel appeared in a dream and assured him that what you had told him—as fantastic and unbelievable as it sounded—was entirely true. Now neither of you are afraid of the gift of this new baby. What you do fear is how others will react to this news. And that's why you have to leave. Immediately.

Thankfully, you have a dear relative, Elizabeth, who, like you, is expecting her first child. Elizabeth and her husband, Zechariah, live in the hill country of Judah, just south and west of Jerusalem. It is close enough for you to travel there quickly and safely but far enough away that you will be shielded from the speculators and slanderers. When Elizabeth welcomes you upon your arrival, both of you are overcome with joy. Her greeting, however, although filled with warmth and love, startles you: "And how does this happen to me," she asks, "that the mother of my Lord should come to me?"

Mother of my Lord? Elizabeth isn't speaking in jest. Her words are shocking; she is calling your child a king. This isn't the first time you've heard this. Gabriel had insisted that your son would be heir to the throne of David, the greatest ruler in your people's history, and of whose line the Messiah—the one who would save God's people—would be born. But if your son is a king, that means that you are a queen mother. This puzzles you. After all, you are a simple peasant girl from an obscure village. You live in a hut, not a palace, and your clothes are rough and simple. Royal families have servants attending to their every need. But no one serves you. Instead, your days are filled with baking, cooking, mending, spinning cloth, drawing water, and tending to your family's few animals. Yes, Joseph is a descendant of David, but he is far from unique. David had lived some six hundred years earlier, after all, and his descendants are not impossible to find. Yet for whatever reason, you are the one whom God chose. All you can do is surrender to the plan, even if you don't understand it.

Just before your child is to be born, you and Joseph have to travel to Bethlehem, his family's hometown. The Roman governor has called for a census, and everyone in Galilee must register in his town of origin. When you arrive, Bethlehem is packed; no lodging can be found anywhere. You have to settle for a stable with buzzing flies, ungracious animals, and the pungent aroma of sweat, urine, and dung. It will have to do. But then your contractions begin. It dawns upon you that you are going to deliver. Here, away from Elizabeth, away from your home, in a shelter suitable only for livestock. Yet there is no other choice; the time has come.

Joseph is encouraging, helpful, and anxious. There is no need to worry, however, as the delivery goes fine. You hold your baby to your chest; your brown eyes meet his, and all is right with the world. Joseph and you then rub him with salt, swaddle him in bands of cloth, and lay him to sleep in a manger—a feeding trough. Filled with straw, the manger actually makes a half-decent crib, as it is slightly inclined and comfortable for a baby's head. Yet it made you laugh, too, as it is totally unsuitable for an infant king. Or so you think, until some unexpected visitors arrive.

You had heard them coming some way off, as they were singing loudly. At first, you think that maybe they are drunk. When they appear at the stable and you see that they are shepherds, you become alarmed. Shepherds have a bad reputation for being untrustworthy ruffians and thieves. Given the nature of their work, many consider shepherds to be unclean and look down upon them with open contempt. Yet these shepherds have an amazing tale to tell. An angel had appeared to them in the fields, proclaiming that the Messiah has just been born and can be found lying in a manger. They become silent as they approach your sleeping child, kneel down, and gaze upon him with wonderment while the world around you seems absolutely silent and still.

This peaceful moment is a revelation for you. These simple people are the first to adore your son as a king. God has picked the humble to seek him out in the most humble of places because God himself is humble. That's why, you understand, that manger is not only suitable for your royal son; it is precisely the place where he is supposed to be. Just then, Joseph turns and looks at you. You take his hand, and the two of you kneel beside the shepherds. You gaze upon Jesus with love as only a mother can. And you know, somehow, that you are in the presence of an even greater love than that.

Days later, your son is formally named Jesus, "God saves." It is a common name, but there is none more fitting. As Jesus grows, you think about his kingship and your being a queen mother. A queen mother's primary responsibility, you know, is to prepare her son for his royal wedding. But Jesus never marries; he doesn't even appear interested in marriage. Plenty of women become his friends, like the sisters Mary and Martha, whom you come to adore. When he journeys from town to town to preach and heal, he includes women as traveling companions. That is unheard of for a rabbi, and it raises a lot of eyebrows. But what raises even more eyebrows is the simple fact that Jesus remains unmarried. It is normal and expected that rabbis marry. But not your son. And so, you conclude, there will be no royal wedding for you to help plan.

But then comes the most horrific day of your life, when you see your son nailed to a cross. In excruciating pain and gasping for each breath, Jesus says few words as he hangs dying. But at one point, he struggles and lifts his head. His eyes meet yours, and then he glances toward his disciple John, who stands beside you. "Woman," he feebly whispers, "behold your son." *Woman?* It is an affectionate term, but one that Jesus has used only once before. When was that? Ah yes—at the wedding party, in Cana. That was three years ago! Jesus and all his disciples were there. It was a lovely party; the entire village rejoiced with the happy, young couple. But as the night progressed, the wine began to run out. You didn't wish for the hosts to be embarrassed, and so you approached your son. "Woman," he asked, "how does your concern affect me? My hour has not yet come."

At the time, you were puzzled by the mention of his "hour," and you wondered why he had addressed you as "woman." But now that he addresses you the same way again, you think that maybe he wants you to associate that wedding and his crucifixion. Yet what possible connection can there be? He had turned water into wine at Cana, but how does that matter now? Your mind races while your thoughts cloud with grief. This is certainly no wedding. There is no bride and no celebration, only mourning and weeping under an increasingly dark sky. You are glad that Jesus had never married, as his wife would likely be grieving alongside you, soon to become a widow.

After three agonizing hours, Jesus utters a pained cry, his head slumps forward, and he dies. While you stand frozen in stunned silence, a soldier steps forward to break his legs so he can't raise himself and fill his lungs. But since Jesus obviously isn't breathing, another soldier instead thrusts a lance into his side to pierce his heart—just in case there is a trace of life in him. Blood pours from the wound. To your amazement, however, water gushes forth, too. At that moment, consumed with loss, you cannot make sense of it at all. It is so unexpected and, as far as you know, unheard of. Nevertheless you realize, even then, that it is deeply significant.

Later, after your son's resurrection, you come to understand that a royal wedding had indeed taken place that day. It hadn't happened as you'd thought it would, but it turned out to be more wonderful than you had ever imagined. Jesus was the royal bridegroom, of course. Even Pilate, the Roman official who had sentenced him to death, had a sign placed on his cross proclaiming him the "King of the Jews." But where was his royal bride? She'd been there, but "she" wasn't an individual woman. Instead, as you would slowly comprehend, "she" was the multitude of women and men who loved your son and, collectively, formed a body—a "bride," if you will.

To you, this now makes perfect sense. Throughout your life, you have been taught that the sacred bond between God and his people—a covenant—is like that of a bridegroom and a bride: permanent, intimate, and loving. After your own marriage to Joseph, you smiled whenever you heard this because it reminded you of the love you shared with him. Now, whenever this image is applied to the covenant between Jesus and his people, you smile again. They call him "Lord," and they will come to call you "Mother." You are, truly, the mother of a king. A queen mother. And you have, indeed, fulfilled your duty of preparing your son for his royal wedding. Even though you hadn't realized it at the time, you had done it at that humble wedding in Cana, when Jesus first called you "woman."

On that lovely day, your son had insisted that his hour had not yet come. You had wondered what this hour referred to and when it might arrive. And then Jesus revealed everything the night before he died, at the Passover meal he celebrated with his disciples. "Father," he prayed, "the hour has come"—the hour of his death, when, with arms outstretched on a cross, he would gather all people in a loving embrace. And in that supreme gesture of love, his bride would be taken from his side just as Eve, Adam's bride, was taken from his. Eve was fashioned from Adam's rib while he slept; your son's bride was born while he slept the sleep of death. But it wasn't a bone from which she was created; it was from the water and blood that gushed forth from the lance's wound. The water represented baptism, through which one becomes united with your son through the same Spirit by which he was conceived in you; the blood signified the wine which the Spirit transforms into Jesus' blood, the blood of the "new covenant," as he called it that Passover night, while he established what you would come to call the Lord's Supper.

Jesus had changed water into wine at Cana at your request. It had amazed you at the time, and it delighted the wedding guests, too. But looking back, you could now appreciate the full significance of what you'd done that day. In prompting Jesus to perform his first sign at that wedding, you set him on the path toward his royal wedding—his crucifixion—at which he would be united with his bride in a covenant of love. There had been no wedding party at the foot of the cross; that would be reserved for heaven, which you'd heard your son describe as a wedding banquet time and time again. But that feast can be tasted just a little bit now, whenever the Lord's Supper is celebrated—when bride and bridegroom are united through bread become body and wine become blood and by a love for which that blood was shed.

Questions
for Journaling, Contemplation, or Conversation

1) In Jesus, God embraced humility and weakness. How does this make you feel? What do you think of this central mystery of our faith?

2) Christian tradition likens the relationship between Jesus and his people to a marriage. Does this influence your understanding of love, commitment, and sacrifice?

Stop and Pray

Holy Mary, Mother of God,
Through his loving embrace from the cross,
I am united with your Son in a new covenant,
as a bride is joined with a bridegroom.
Pray that our bond grows ever deeper,
as I await the glorious wedding feast of heaven.
Amen.

Going Deeper

. . . .

Luke 1:26–38	Gabriel's Annunciation to Mary
Luke 1:39–45	Mary's Visit to Elizabeth
Matthew 1:18–25	Joseph's Dream
Luke 2:1–14	The Birth of Jesus
Luke 2:15–21	Shepherds Visit the Infant Jesus
Luke 8:1–3	Women Accompany Jesus
Song of Songs 3:11	Queen Mothers and Royal Weddings
Luke 10:38–42; John 11:1–44	Jesus' Friendship with Mary and Martha
John 2:1–12	The Wedding at Cana
John 19:25–27	Jesus Calls Mary "Woman" from the Cross
John 19:31–37	Wine and Water Pour Forth from Jesus' Side
Genesis 2:21–24	Eve Taken from Adam's Side
Matthew 22:1–2	Heaven Described as a Wedding Banquet
Matthew 26:28–29	Blood of the Covenant and the Lord's Supper

6. MATTHEW

Forgiveness

Who was St. Matthew?

As a former tax collector who became an apostle, St. Matthew was a living testament to the mercy Jesus preached. While no person is beyond God's mercy, it required great sacrifice and humility for Matthew to turn away from the wealth and power that came with his position. Tax collectors were protected by the Romans for whom they worked but despised by the people who paid taxes. This was certainly true for Matthew in his hometown of Capernaum. Animosity from neighbors, however, may have contributed to Matthew's conversion after a simple invitation from Jesus: "Follow me." After the Resurrection, tradition states that he took the Gospel to Ethiopia. It is possible that Matthew was married.

• • • • • •

Few people in your hometown of Capernaum will actually look you in the eye, let alone have a conversation with you. You are a tax collector, and aside from your fellow tax collectors and a handful of equally wealthy friends, you are essentially an outcast. It is your own fault; you realize that. No one forced you to become a tax collector. When the opportunity to bid on the position of collecting taxes for the Romans presented itself, you jumped at the chance, and given your already ample resources, you won the spot. Your responsibility is to collect a predetermined sum to hand over to your Roman superior; anything collected over and above that amount is yours to keep. After meeting your obligation, you are accountable to no one but yourself, and you have no qualms whatsoever about squeezing every last shekel out of your fellow Jews, not to mention the merchants who come to and from Damascus in the northeast, bearing silk and spices and returning with dried fish and fruits. Over time, you have become very rich indeed. And over that same time, your neighbors have come to scorn you and hold you in contempt.

That's why you were not invited to Peter's house the day something happened which had the entire town talking. It involved Jesus, a rabbi from nearby Nazareth, who had recently relocated to Capernaum. Not long after his arrival, he had begun to teach in public, and crowds from seemingly every quarter came to hear him. You yourself didn't do so. Nevertheless, you couldn't help but hear about Jesus and the impact he was making. Capernaum is a city with only about 1,500 residents. Secrets are hard enough to keep in such a small community, and the excitement caused by the sensational new neighbor quickly reached even your ears. Among other things, you learned that Jesus called two pairs of brothers to be his followers: Peter and Andrew and James and John. All four are fishermen. They are not your friends, but they certainly know who you are, as you've taxed their catches of fish and loaned them money to buy their boats. They still owe you money. Quite a bit, actually.

In fact, a good number of people owe you money, especially the farmers. Their ancestral plots of land are so small and their crop yields so inadequate that they barely grow enough food to live on, let alone pay their taxes. And so they borrow, and borrow, and borrow some more until their debt loads become so heavy that you will eventually foreclose on their properties, leaving them landless, jobless, and enraged at you and everyone with whom you associate. Many of them will become day laborers, working in fields that perhaps had once been legally theirs but are now owned by wealthy landlords who acquire foreclosed farms from tax collectors like you. Some of those landlords you count among your small handful of friends. Yet none of the dispossessed peasant farmers is your friend. Those farmers, however, appear to be greatly attracted to Jesus; sometimes you see them go out in droves to hear him speak.

Part of you wonders what the fascination is all about. Is Jesus a revolutionary? A prophet? Or another opportunistic charlatan? You are curious, as nothing like this has ever happened in Capernaum. Yes, your town is located on a major road, the *Via Maris*, but outsiders usually come only to trade or pass through. But now that Jesus has appeared, visitors are arriving from all over Galilee, the Decapolis, Jerusalem, Judea, and even beyond the Jordan River. This, in and of itself, has generated quite a bit of buzz. Yet, it is what Jesus does that creates more of a stir. One Sabbath, he taught in the town synagogue. His teaching, you later came to learn, had been deeply impressive and delivered with an authority that people were unused to hearing. However, it was Jesus' casting out an unclean spirit who had accused him of being the "Holy One of God" that filled everyone with amazement and caused his fame to spread.

You have witnessed none of this, of course. Even if you had wanted to see Jesus in the synagogue that day, you wouldn't have been permitted inside. That is a consequence of your choice of profession. When you became a tax collector, you were effectively shunned by your fellow Jews from that point forward. In particular, it is the Pharisees—those who claim to uphold the highest standards of righteousness—who fan the flames of animosity toward the likes of you. Thanks to their teaching, you are publicly condemned as a "sinner." They insist that a house becomes religiously "unclean" by your very presence. Other Jews are not permitted to trade, eat, or pray with you, and you are forbidden to enter synagogues or sacrifice in the great Temple in Jerusalem.

Tax collecting has filled your coffers handsomely. Over time, however, it has led first to increasing loneliness and isolation and later to deep-rooted guilt and shame. Almost all of your neighbors and fellow kinsman have come to hate you. You have even come to hate yourself. After all you've done, and the enemies you've created, there is seemingly no turning back from your current way of life. You've considered moving elsewhere, but what would you do? All you know is tax collecting, and your sedentary work has made you unfit for more strenuous labor. Besides, you are too proud to stoop that low, and relocating will simply involve creating a new set of enemies. In addition, there is no guarantee that you could be a tax collector elsewhere, as those jobs go to the highest bidders, and high bidders typically have connections in high places. You feel trapped, which has caused you to become angry, and you've vented your rage on those from whom you've collected taxes. Most recently, you've shown them no mercy whatsoever. What would be the point? Showing mercy won't make them like you more, as you are shunned whether you collect excess taxes or only what the government requires. And you are certain that God will show you no mercy. You crossed that point of no return long, long ago.

Or so you thought, until today, when you heard a report of something Jesus did that is unlike anything you—or anyone else—has heard of before. Jesus had been teaching in Peter's home. A great crowd filled the house so that it was wall-to-wall with people. Four friends of a paralyzed man came in hope that Jesus would heal him, but since they couldn't squeeze him through the door, they lowered him down through the roof instead. To everyone's disbelief, Jesus healed the man, who was able to walk home with joy. But even more astonishing was that Jesus declared that this man's sins had been forgiven. As even you know full well, only God himself can forgive sins. The Pharisees were outraged at Jesus for this and made their objections quite clear. You, however, aren't scandalized at all. At first, you are intrigued. But the more you reflect on it, you begin to experience the beginnings of hope. Because, you realize, you have come to want God's forgiveness more than anything else.

Now you are back working at your customs post, feeling more guilty and trapped than ever, when a crowd passes by. It isn't a merchant caravan returning to Syria; it is Jesus and his followers. You recognize most of them. Several owe you money, and a few you've forced into bankruptcy; all of them know who you are, and none dare look you in the eye. Except Jesus. He catches your gaze, and to your relief, his eyes are filled with compassion, not contempt. So when he extends a simple invitation, "Follow me," you do not hesitate for a moment. You leave your customs post behind. You leave your very way of life behind. But you sense that you are moving into a new life, one of fresh beginnings and, most of all, of mercy and forgiveness.

This evening, you host a great banquet for Jesus at your house. Many of your fellow tax collectors join you, as do others who have been publicly labeled as sinners. Jesus seems comfortable and happy dining alongside all of you. But certain prying Pharisees are scandalized and complain out loud, wondering how on earth Jesus can, as they say, "eat with tax collectors and sinners." Jesus overheard them; in fact they want him to, as they are itching for a fight or at least a heated argument. However, Jesus turns a contentious moment into a teachable one by issuing a stern but compassionate challenge: "Go and learn the meaning of the words," he insists, "'I desire mercy, not sacrifice.'" From that moment on, you know that mercy is at the heart of all Jesus says and does. If he can extend mercy to the likes of you, then no one is exempt. And it all began in your home and at your table.

You aren't the only tax collector Jesus has singled out for special attention. Zacchaeus of Jericho, who will become a dear friend, is another. Notorious for his dishonesty and lack of scruples, Zacchaeus is extremely rich, but years of scorn and contempt from the wider community have taken its toll. Like you, he has come to desperately long for hope, acceptance, love, and mercy. And also like you, he will find it in Jesus, who will pick Zaccheus out from a crowd and insist on visiting his home. You are excited to witness this, but those surrounding you are disgusted and wonder out loud why Jesus would have anything to do with such a "sinner." Your heart sinks when you hear these words, but then it leaps with joy when Zacchaeus promises to right his past wrongs and Jesus announces that the man has found salvation. Referring to himself, Jesus explains that he has "come to seek and to save what was lost."

After becoming friends, you and Zacchaeus discuss a parable Jesus taught about two debtors who owed great sums of money to a creditor—quite possibly also a tax collector! With regret, you both recall the countless individuals who have been indebted to you and whose pleas for mercy fell on deaf ears. In Jesus' story, however, the creditor forgave both debts, just as Jesus has forgiven the two of you. Jesus concluded the tale by saying that he is loved by those who have known his forgiveness. And you couldn't agree more. You love Jesus for having loved you when no one else did, when you couldn't even love yourself. Given your wealth, you have owned many precious possessions in your lifetime, but by embracing you with acceptance, mercy, and forgiveness, Jesus has given you something money can't buy and a gift far more precious than anything you have ever known before. You wonder if Jesus has this in mind when he gives you a new name on becoming an apostle. Your parents had named you Levi, but Jesus calls you Matthew, "Gift of the Lord."

Often, you recall that this precious gift of forgiveness was first given to you at the table in your own house, when Jesus happily dined with you and other "sinners." The image of that meal enters your mind as you dine at another table, for a Passover meal with Jesus and your fellow apostles, hours before he is arrested. Jesus takes his cup of wine and to everyone's surprise, calls it his "blood." He next passes his cup to everyone, explaining that his blood will be shed "for the forgiveness of sins." Then he insists, "Do this in memory of me." In time, you will come to appreciate that those words were intended not just to recall a forgiveness given then and there but to extend that forgiveness anew, over and over again, at each and every table around which that Passover meal is repeated at what you and your friends come to call the Lord's Supper. You will know that the forgiveness Jesus came to bring, and for which he shed his blood, was a gift not just for you and your companions but for "sinners" of every time and place.

As the years pass after Jesus returns to his Father, you will celebrate the Lord's Supper with other followers of Jesus as your fellowship expands—first with other Jews, and later, far to the south in Ethiopia, where you will journey to spread the good news of Jesus' forgiveness—and where you will end your days. You will witness countless people come to Jesus as you once did—broken in spirit, devoid of hope, thinking themselves unlovable and conscious of their failings—only to discover not rejection and condemnation but respect, love, and forgiveness. You will smile whenever they do, rejoicing that Jesus once rejoiced to dine with the likes of you. And that he still does.

Questions
for Journaling, Contemplation, or Conversation

1) Has there been a time when you felt helpless or lost? How did you respond to the situation and to your feelings?

2) What has been your experience of forgiveness? What lessons have you gleaned from it?

Stop and Pray

Holy Jesus,
My sins separate me from others and from you.
They can paralyze me with guilt and shame,
yet you came to seek and save what was lost.
Thank you for welcoming me to your table
and filling me with your mercy.
Amen.

Going Deeper

Matthew 4:25	Crowds from Afar Hear Jesus in Jerusalem
Matthew 4:18–22	Jesus Calls Four Capernaum Fishermen as Disciples
Matthew 7:28–29	Astonishment at Jesus' Teaching
Mark 1:21–22	Jesus Teaches in Capernaum Synagogue
Mark 1:23–28	Man with Unclean Spirit Cured by Jesus
Matthew 9:1–8	Paralyzed Man Healed and Forgiven by Jesus

7. Peter

Unity

Who was St. Peter?

St. Peter was a fisherman from Galilee, as was his brother Andrew. He was raised with the name Simon, but Jesus named him Peter, or "rock," and established him as leader of his band of twelve disciples. While Jesus was on trial, Peter denied knowing him three times, as Jesus had predicted. After the Resurrection, however, Peter would strengthen the faith of many, first in Jerusalem and later in Rome. Tradition recalls that Peter established new churches throughout Lebanon where, according to one account, he met with St. Paul in the city of Sidon before Paul began his final missionary journey. Both men would later die in Rome for their faith.

• • • • • •

You, your fellow disciples, and Jesus have journeyed north to Sidon, on the coast of the Great Sea. This is the farthest you have ever ventured from your childhood home in Galilee. After all, you have been a fisherman your whole life and have never really had a need, let alone an opportunity, to travel. Before you met Jesus, your only travels had been visits to Jerusalem to celebrate Passover. Jerusalem was exciting, to be sure, and you sometimes felt a little apprehensive there, but it seemed comfortable and familiar at the same time because you were surrounded by fellow Jews. You spoke the same language, worshiped the same God, and shared the same traditions. You felt at home there even if the city dwellers did sometimes tease you for your rural accent. Once you had ordered sheep's feet for dinner and were served lentils instead—a confusion caused by your mispronouncing a single syllable!

Being in Sidon, however, feels entirely different. There are certainly Jews here; it is to them that Jesus has come to speak of the kingdom of God. But unlike Jerusalem, Sidon is not a Jewish city. Historically, it has been Phoenician and a center of trade for goods coming and going to distant ports around the Great Sea. The Phoenicians are skilled seafarers, and five centuries earlier, Sidon had been their most important city. Its glory has faded a bit since then, having been overshadowed in importance by Tyre—its sister and rival city some thirty-five miles to the south. Nevertheless, Sidon still flourishes and is renowned for its glassworks and purple-dyed textiles, which are coveted by the wealthy. Being a seaport, it is also a major center of the fishing trade. This being your first visit to Sidon, you enjoy watching the fishermen offshore, expertly working the coastal waters.

Along with you, three other disciples are also fishermen: James and John, who are brothers, and your own brother, Andrew. In fact, long before any of you began to follow Jesus, the four of you worked in a fishing cooperative to pool your resources and buy boats and other essential tools of your craft. During your brief visit to Sidon, the four of you watch in fascination as the local fishermen haul in their catches by daylight, and you admire their seamanship in the heavy swells. You yourself are a lake fisherman, but you know what it is like to fight rough seas, as the Galilee lake you worked could be subjected to fierce windstorms. Nevertheless, the open sea frightens you. Historically, Jews haven't been mariners, and in the scriptures and legends you've heard your whole life, the sea is associated with chaos, monsters, and death. You are impressed by the courage of the Sidonian fishermen and intrigued that they work while the sun is up. You've done your fishing at night, for by day, the fish you've sought to catch would descend to the bottom of the lake where the water is cooler and predators could not see them. Over the years, they have provided you with a good living with which to care for your family.

Some of the fish you caught in Galilee ended up in Sidon, having been salted and transported there by merchants. That's why, when you and Andrew are in the city market one morning to buy provisions for your group, you ask the fishmongers if any of their stock might have originated from your hometown. You are disappointed that none of them know or really even care, but you are impressed by the variety of seafood they offer. There are any number of kinds of fish, but what especially catch your eye are the shellfish: mussels, oysters, and shrimp. You have heard about such creatures, but you have never before seen them, let alone eaten them, for they are considered to be unclean; God had specifically forbidden them from the Jewish diet. "Whatever in the seas or in river waters that has both fins and scales you may eat," you knew from the scriptures. "But of the creatures that swarm in the water . . . all those that lack either fins or scales are loathsome for you." Although you have observed that commandment your whole life, it hasn't been terribly difficult to do as there are no edible shellfish harvested in Galilee. And even if there were, no pious Jew would even consider serving them. Still, as you gaze at these curiosities in the Sidon market, you conclude that some people must enjoy them, and you wonder what they taste like.

On a visit to Sidon years later, you get your chance. This time, you are in the city to meet with Paul, a fellow Christian leader, with whom you have had a long mutual history. Paul hadn't known Jesus during his lifetime and therefore wasn't one of his initial followers. In fact, at one time he had taken it upon himself to stamp out any and all Christians—you included. But then Jesus appeared to him while he was traveling and changed the direction of his life forever. Paul was baptized and, almost overnight, became as passionate an advocate for Jesus as he had once been an opponent. Surprisingly, given his lifelong zeal for Jewish traditions, his ministry is directed toward those who aren't Jews. Instead, he firmly believes that he has a special mandate to preach the Gospel to the Gentiles, as Jews call them. In time, Paul has come to identify himself as the "apostle to the Gentiles."

Paul teaches that Gentiles who become Christian don't need to observe traditional Jewish laws, such as circumcision for men or restrictions against eating shellfish. It is by faith that one is saved, he insists, and not through the keeping of rules. Paul's approach has been welcomed in some quarters but has met with resistance in others. You understand those who are hesitant because you once struggled with this question yourself. Preaching to the Gentiles is not the issue. After all, Jesus' parting commandment was for his followers to go throughout all the earth and "make disciples of all nations," not simply fellow Jews. You had taken this to heart. How could you not? And then there was your experience in Jerusalem during the feast of Pentecost, not long after Jesus had ascended into heaven, when the Holy Spirit was poured out upon you and the other disciples with tongues of fire and a mighty rush of wind. Driven by the Spirit, you rushed out to preach to the crowds, who were astounded that everyone who listened was able to understand you in his or her native tongue. The miracle you witnessed that day was a confirmation that Jesus' message, and the salvation he promised, was intended for everyone.

However, Jesus' wanting his good news preached to the Gentiles didn't mean that those who embraced it were exempt from Jewish laws. Those were sacred traditions that helped Jews remember that they were God's people. Traditions were precious to you, especially those you'd observed since childhood, and you understood keeping them as essential to your relationship with God. Regarding food, you recalled that Jesus himself had said that nothing that enters a person from the outside can make him or her unclean. But lifelong habits can become deeply ingrained. Yet your thinking changed during a visit to the port town of Joppa, while staying in the home of Simon, a tanner. You had climbed atop the flat roof to pray in solitude and received a vision of a great sheet descending from heaven, filled with every sort of animal, reptile, and bird. A voice invited you: "Slaughter and eat." Even though you were hungry, you declined, insisting that you had never eaten anything Jewish law considered unclean. Nevertheless, in order to dispel your doubt, the voice insisted three times that God now declared all food to be clean. Including those shellfish in the Sidon market.

The very next day, you found yourself dining in a Gentile home, and you gladly ate all that was served. But in spite of your new convictions, controversy about observing Jewish laws would rage on within the church. As leader of the apostles, you received pressure from those on both sides of the debate, and the strain became so great that for a time you reverted to your old ways. Matters came to a head when Paul arrived in Jerusalem to seek confirmation from the church's authorities about his teachings. At an assembly, powerful voices insisted that all the old laws must be kept. After they had made their case, every eye turned to you, and a vivid memory of your vision at Joppa filled you with courage to speak about what you had witnessed God doing with the Gentiles. "He made no distinction between us and them," you insisted, as it was through faith, not the keeping of laws, that God had "purified their hearts." Paul was vindicated, and all those gathered listened in rapt silence as he spoke of how God had been blessing his ministry.

Ten years passed, and you found yourself back in Sidon, this time to meet with Paul, who was just beginning an ambitious missionary journey. Sidon was familiar to you by then, as you had visited several times while you established new churches throughout Lebanon. The highlight of this visit was when you, Paul, and the entire Christian community celebrated the Lord's Supper together. As you led the prayers, you surveyed the faces of those gathered around you. You knew many of their names and where they were from. Because Sidon was a seaport, the church there included men and women from far and wide: Egypt, Persia, Crete, Asia, Mesopotamia, Greece, Libya, Italy, and even Gaul and Spain. Some had been raised Jewish, but most were born Gentile. The diversity of the group reminded you of Paul's unwavering assertion that what unites sisters and brothers has nothing to do with what foods they may or may not eat. Paul was careful to make one qualification to his teaching, however; while Jewish food laws were not binding for Christians, it was a *meal* that bound Christians together: the very Lord's Supper you were leading. As Paul himself had written, "Because the loaf of bread is one, we, though many, are one body, for we all partake of the one loaf."

After the Lord's Supper that evening, the community remained for a meal; a "love feast," they called it. Everyone brought something to share so no one would leave hungry. Someone brought shrimp from the local market—the same market you had visited while with

Jesus years before. It had been boiled and seasoned, and you were pleased to help yourself. After peeling off its shell, you ate one whole and savored a taste denied to you for much of your life, a taste you had come to love. A verse from the Psalms came to mind: "How good and how pleasant it is, when brothers dwell together as one!" You chuckled to yourself and thought, "How good it is for brothers and sisters to dine together with food like this!" And even better, you concluded, to be one in Christ at the supper of the Lord.

Questions
for Journaling, Contemplation, or Conversation

1) Does your faith shape the way you view and approach people of different cultures and backgrounds?

2) In your faith life, are you overall more comfortable with traditional practices or new ones? Has your preference ever been challenged? If so, in what ways?

Stop and Pray

Christ Jesus, savior of all,
You commission us to make disciples of all nations;
it is good and pleasant when brothers and sisters
dwell together as one.
We are many as we gather around your table,
and I am grateful that you unite me with my fellow
disciples into one body.
Amen.

Going Deeper

Mark 7:24–32	Peter, Jesus, and the Apostles in Sidon
Mark 1:16–20	Peter, Andrew, James, and John as Fishermen
Mark 4:35–41	Sea of Galilee Subject to Storms
Psalm 74:13–15 Psalm 33:6–7 Isaiah 27:1	Seas Associated with Chaos, Monsters, and Death
Luke 5:5 John 21:3	Night Fishing on the Sea of Galilee
Leviticus 11:9–12	Shellfish Designated as Unclean
Romans 11:13	Paul Is Apostle to the Gentiles
Romans 14:14	All Food Is Acceptable for Christians
Ephesians 2:8–9	Salvation through Faith, Not Observing Rules
Matthew 28:19	Make Disciples of All Nations
Acts 2:1–41	Peter's Preaching on Pentecost
Mark 7:15	Nothing from Outside Defiles a Person
Acts 10:9–23	Peter's Vision in Joppa
Acts 15:1–12	Peter at the Council of Jerusalem
1 Corinthians 10:17	Christians United through One Loaf
Jude 12	Love Feasts at Early Christian Gatherings
Psalm 133:1	Dwelling in Unity as Good and Pleasant

8. Mark

Remembrance

Who was St. Mark?

By ancient accounts, the authorship of what is likely the oldest of the four gospels is attributed to St. Mark. Although Mark was not one of the original twelve apostles, he was certainly an early follower of Jesus. The gospel that bears his name tells of a young man who fled naked from the scene of Jesus' arrest, and it has been suggested that this young man was Mark himself. It is further speculated that the Last Supper was celebrated in the upper room of his family's home, which became a meeting place for the apostles after the Resurrection. Later, Mark became a traveling companion of Peter, whose preaching is said to have formed the basis of Mark's gospel. Finally, Mark has long been honored as the traditional founder of the church in Alexandria, Egypt.

• • • • • •

After months of work—thinking, reflecting, composing, editing, rearranging—your project is nearing completion. You have been writing about Jesus of Nazareth, the Son of God, because you want to tell his story to the world. The people who knew him while he walked the earth are passing from the scene. Some have died from natural causes; that is to be expected, as Jesus himself had left—ascended into heaven, actually—some thirty years ago. Many more have been killed for being his followers, however, and it is quite possible that you will meet the same fate. You feel an urgency to write about Jesus so those who come after you can truly understand who he is and what he did and can come to embrace the good news he preached. In fact, you have wondered if Jesus himself, through the Holy Spirit, has nudged you to start this project and has somehow been helping you along.

Today, you have been writing quickly; words flow freely as your reed pen scratches furiously on the papyrus scroll before you. You have been describing the events of that last, terrible night before Jesus was crucified, and you have reached the point where armed guards arrested him and his disciples abandoned him. "And they all left him and fled," you write, but then your pen freezes. Should you include what happened next? After all, it isn't an essential part of the story. It concerns a young man who had been watching the events unfold while hiding in the shadows. A guard with a torch had spotted him, however, and that guard and a companion ran to catch him. In spite of their armor and weapons, they were surprisingly fast, and one managed to grab the young man's cloak. With a deft twist, he escaped, but his cloak was torn away, forcing him to flee into the darkness entirely naked.

Why include such a detail? Because you were that young man; you yourself were an eyewitness to the earth-shattering, history-making events you are now describing. It isn't a second- or third-hand account you are passing on. To be sure, there was much of Jesus' ministry that you hadn't been part of, as you weren't one of his twelve disciples. But you had been there for some of it, especially the fateful climax of Jesus' life. Should you include the episode of your running away into the night? Yes, you conclude, so your readers will know that you aren't spinning a fanciful tale. You want to ensure they understand that what you are writing is true. More than anything, you want them to remember all that Jesus really said and did.

The events of that night are seared in your memory. It was Passover, the ancient Jewish celebration of God freeing the Israelites, your ancestors, from cruel slavery in Egypt. At the evening supper, what God had done for his people was remembered through traditions, teachings, prayers, and songs. However, the Passover meal was more than simply a recollection of an event from long ago. Rather, it was understood that, in some way, this ancient event was made present again. It was as if all of the guests at that meal were being freed from slavery by God just as their forebears had been centuries before. At Passover, the past wasn't just remembered; it was experienced.

Just before his arrest, Jesus had eaten the Passover meal at your own home in Jerusalem. Days earlier, he had sent you special instructions through a messenger: on the day of the meal, you were to meet two of his disciples in the city streets, carrying a water jar so they could recognize you. They would then follow you to your house, where the upper room would be prepared for the feast. You were honored to have been given such a mission by Jesus and that, of all the places he could have chosen, he and his disciples were going to celebrate Passover under your very roof.

Since then, you had worked hard to prepare for your guests. The evening before, you had searched high and low for any morsels of leavened bread, burning what you found. This traditional practice, which all your neighbors observed as well, was a reminder that when God led the Israelites from Egypt, they had to eat unleavened bread because, in their haste to flee, there had been no time to allow yeast to rise. The following

morning, you and thousands of others made your way
through the city to the great Temple atop Mount Zion, its
gold leaf blazing so brightly in the sunlight that you had
to avert your eyes. Inside the Temple was a cacophony
of horn blasts, chanting priests, and bleating sheep and
goats. You yourself had a sheep that, when you arrived
at the high altar, you slaughtered with a quick slit to
the throat. It was then butchered by the priests, after
which you took the meat home to roast on skewers of
pomegranate wood.

In addition to cooking the lamb, there was a great
deal of other food to prepare. Thankfully, your mother,
Mary, and some of her friends were available to assist
with that. They stewed lentils and beans, baked unleavened bread, mixed dates and nuts into a chunky paste
called *haroset,* and arranged what were called the "bit-
ter herbs," or *maror*: parsley, chicory, hawkweed, and
sow-thistles. This maror was meant to recall the bit-
terness of slavery in Egypt. It would be eaten with the
lamb along with the haroset, which recalled the mortar
used by the Israelites to make bricks for their Egyptian
masters. As for the lamb, it was what God had instructed
your ancestors to eat at the very first Passover, back in
the time of Moses.

While your mother and her friends worked, you had
been busy readying the room upstairs. Cushions had
to be arranged in a semi-circle around the low wooden
table, which you set with plates, bowls, and cups made
of stone. Like all the other dining tables you had seen,
yours was only knee-height, allowing your guests to
lean on their left elbows and eat with their right hands.
From time to time, you'd hear reports of higher tables
at which people sat upright in chairs, but this sounded
odd to you. After all, eating while reclined helped with
digestion, and resting on cushions made dining a leisurely affair. This was only fitting, as sharing a meal
with others was a sign of acceptance and respect and

should therefore never be rushed. As your own sign of respect, you planned for Jesus to be placed at the table's corner, as he would be the most distinguished person present.

When Jesus and his companions arrived at sundown, you were ecstatic. Passover was a festive celebration, and spirits were usually high. Your guests' faces, however, reflected a different mood. Jesus was gracious, but he appeared solemn. As you would learn later, he knew that he would be betrayed by a friend that very night. His disciples looked downcast as well and seemed terribly anxious. The tension in the air was thick, and for good reason. Jesus had been warning his disciples about the great dangers and persecutions they would face. Your friend Peter seemed especially grave. You asked him quietly if you might join him and the others for the meal, but he simply shook his head and slowly ascended the stairs.

Now feeling sad, you ate your Passover meal downstairs with your mother, her friends, and a handful of other followers of Jesus. Your companions seemed happy enough, and the four cups of wine they consumed by custom livened the mood. For you, however, the wine only further depressed your spirits. You were concerned about Jesus and the disciples, and you desperately wanted to know what was happening in the room above you. At one point, the disciple Judas, looking ashen but determined, bounded down the stairs and rushed into the night without acknowledging anyone. You stared after him in stunned disbelief, but nobody from upstairs came down to explain what was going on. And so, as best you could, you strained to hear whatever snippets of conversation could be picked up through the ceiling.

It was hard to hear anything, of course, as a Passover meal was a typically noisy affair. However, during those few moments when your table companions were

silently eating, you caught faint, muffled echoes of what
was taking place in your upper room. There was the
creaking of wood, the clattering of plates and bowls, a
stray cough. Sometimes, when all the disciples spoke
excitedly at once, you couldn't hear what was being
said. When the traditional *Hallel* or "Praise" psalms were
recited, it was obvious what was taking place, even if
you couldn't detect all the words. At one point, however,
the psalm text "The Lord remembers us and will bless
us" came through distinctly. You smiled when James and
John's voices rose above the others; there was a reason
Jesus had nicknamed them "Sons of Thunder." Later
you heard, "When Israel came forth from Egypt, the
house of Jacob from an alien people . . ." Matthew's
voice was clearest then; no one was more proud of being
a Jew than he. Finally, there was a moment when Jesus'
voice was heard alone, and it seemed as if his disciples
were utterly and reverently silent. "Do this," he said,
"in memory of me."

The command intrigued and baffled you because
it was certainly not a part of the normal Passover proceedings. You did not know what Jesus was speaking
about, but you sensed that he was asking his friends
to remember something of immense importance. But
what, exactly? In the snatches of psalms you had heard
from upstairs, God had been asked to remember his
people, and God's people were reminded of what God
had done for them. Jesus, however, wanted something
he had done to be remembered, and you had no clue as
to what it could be. Was it the time he walked on water?
Blessed the children? Raised the little girl from the dead?
Fed the crowds with a handful of loaves and fishes? All
you could do was speculate; an answer to your question
would have to wait.

It wasn't until three days later that you learned what
Jesus wanted remembered. You were back in your upper
room, as it was there that the disciples gathered after

Jesus died. The tables and cushions were still arranged
as they had been at Passover; in your grief, you hadn't
rearranged anything. You spoke with Peter, who
explained through tears how Jesus, during the meal,
had blessed and broken unleavened bread, said "Take
it; this is my body," and then passed around his own
cup of wine, which to everyone's shock he identified as
his "blood." It was then that he said, "Do this in memory of me." When Jesus was crucified the following day
and the frightened disciples heard how his body was
nailed to a cross and his life's blood poured forth, they
concluded that Jesus had given this commandment so
his death would never be forgotten. You had to agree;
it made perfect sense.

You were right, as it turned out. Jesus did want his
death to be remembered by eating his body and drinking his blood. But as you would come to understand
later, he had intended much more than that. Not only
did he wish for his death to be remembered but his
resurrection, too, since his body and blood, so horribly
separated at his death, were again united when he rose
to new life. And being a Jew, you knew what remem-
bering involved: a past event made present again, as the
Passover became present again for those who ate and
drank the Passover Meal. So, too, with the Lord's Supper, as it became called: those who ate and drank Jesus'
body and blood didn't simply remember his death and
resurrection. Instead, these events were made present
again so that the benefits of what Jesus accomplished
through them could be extended to people of every time
and place. The Passover liberated God's people from
slavery; the Lord's Supper liberated God's people from
sin and death.

Jesus' insistence that his greatest acts be remembered by eating his body and drinking his blood was
the only thing he asked be done for his own sake. You
smile to think that he made this request under your own

roof, and you smile again as you write of running away
naked earlier that same night, as horrible as it was. After
writing this, words again flow freely from your hand,
and you quickly bring your composition to a close. Your
urgency to tell Jesus' story makes you glad to be done,
but you are consoled in knowing that even if you had
never finished, Jesus would best be remembered not
through any effort of yours but by faithfulness to his
command: "Do this in memory of me."

Questions
for Journaling, Contemplation, or Conversation

1) In the Eucharist, it's understood that the past is made
   present. What do you think of this? Can you make
   sense of it?

2) Along your journey of faith, what have been your
   most memorable experiences? What makes them so?

Stop and Pray

Redeeming Lord,
To liberate us from sin and death,
you offered your body and shed your blood on the
cross.
May I never forget your act of sacrificial love,
and continue to extend its benefits and blessing
to all those I meet
through obedience to your command,
"Do this in memory of me."
Amen.

Going Deeper

....

Mark 14:43–52	Naked Man Flees at Jesus' Arrest
Mark 14:12–16	Jesus' Disciples Prepare for Passover
Exodus 12:1–28, 43–49 Leviticus 23:4–14 Numbers 9:2–5	Jewish Passover Traditions
Mark 14:17–26	The Last Supper
Psalm 114–118	Psalms Sung during Passover Meals
Luke 22:19	"Do This in Memory of Me"
I Corinthians 11:20	Eucharist Referred to as the "Lord's Supper"

9. SIMON

peace

Who was St. Simon?

To follow Jesus during his ministry required passion, energy, and commitment. In a word: zeal. St. Simon possessed all these characteristics; twice, scripture refers to him as a "zealot." This may indicate that he was a member of the Jewish zealot movement, whose activities were characterized by aggression and violence against the occupying Romans. A bellicose edge to his personality is suggested by his having asked, "Lord, shall we strike with a sword?" when Jesus was confronted by arresting soldiers. But regardless of whether Simon was associated with this group prior to his conversion, he certainly helped to spread the Good News of Jesus with great zeal. After the Resurrection, Simon became closely associated with St. Jude, a fellow apostle, with whom tradition says he became a missionary to Persia and Armenia.

• • • • • •

The donkey stands tied to a post, just as Jesus had said it would be. An obviously young colt, he isn't an impressive animal: dusty and gray with long pointed ears, sturdy but comically stubby legs, and shoulders that come only to your chest. He eyes you casually as you

approach, and his ears, low and to the side, indicate
that he is relaxed. You advance slowly, holding out your
hand for him to smell, which he does. Disappointed that
you aren't offering a treat, he raises his head with indifference but allows you to stroke his nose and scratch his
ears. As you begin to untie his lead rope, his owners,
Malachi and Rachel, appear at your left. You are startled,
but they aren't hostile. In fact, it seems as if they have
been expecting your arrival.

"Why are you untying this colt?" asks Malachi. It
isn't a demand; it is a prearranged code phrase, given
earlier by Jesus himself, and for which Malachi expects
to hear a predetermined answer.

"The Master has need of it," you reply, correctly.
On hearing this, Malachi smiles and finishes untying
the lead rope for you. Meanwhile, Rachel brings you a
second donkey: somewhat bigger, and evidently older;
the colt's mother. As you will later learn, her little colt
has never been ridden before, and Rachel is wise enough
to have his mother accompany him with you so he will
feel safe and secure.

As you and Jude, a fellow disciple and your companion for the day, lead the pair from Bethphage back
to Bethany where Jesus is staying, you puzzle over why
Jesus would have need of these donkeys. Donkeys are
beasts of burden, after all. Perhaps he wants them to
carry provisions you are unaware of. But that seems
unlikely. Jesus always travels lightly and insists that his
followers do so as well; a cloak, a staff, and sandals are
all that he typically permits. For a fleeting moment, you
think that maybe Jesus wants to ride one of them. But
that ridiculous notion brings a grin to your face as you
quickly swat that thought away. The only people who
ride donkeys are children, women, and the weak and
frail. Certainly not Jesus, who is strong and accustomed
to walking great distances. Men like him ride a horse,
not an ass.

But not today, as you soon see. Along with thousands of pilgrims from far and wide, Jesus is preparing to enter Jerusalem for the feast of Passover to celebrate how, centuries earlier, God had freed your ancestors from slavery in Egypt. In one sense, this is nothing new; Jesus has been to Jerusalem for Passover many times before. This year, however, Jesus' arrival has been anticipated by the crowds, and he doesn't wish for it to be misunderstood. His teaching and miracles have aroused great excitement that he might be the Messiah, the longed-for descendant of David, the great Jewish warrior-king of centuries before. Many hope that the Messiah will lead his people in revolt against the Romans and free the Jews from their oppressive yoke. They long for a hero, a champion, someone who will enter the city on horseback and in armor, inspiring courage and awe. You yourself have entertained this hope for Jesus. When you first met him, you had been a "zealot"—a passionate, young Jewish man eager to fight the Romans and restore the liberty—and the glory—of your people.

Since then, Jesus has dashed your expectations time and again, challenging your understanding of who the Messiah is and what he will do. You were challenged again this very day when he specifically sent you to fetch the young colt and her mother. Jesus knows that, deep in your heart, you still harbor a desire to fight and live by the sword, and he has been trying to soften that heart. When you present the colt to Jesus, he thanks you, smiles, and pats the young animal's neck. He then asks your help in mounting the little beast because, he explains, he will ride it into the city. Initially, you are shocked and about to protest. But then it dawns on you: Jesus is a king, and for a king to approach a city on a donkey is an intentional act of humility, indicating that he approaches in peace. A passage from scripture springs to mind: "Exult greatly, O daughter Zion! Shout for joy, O daughter Jerusalem! Behold: your king is coming to you, a just savior is he, humble, and riding on a donkey, on a colt, the foal of a donkey."

At that moment, your eyes widen and you draw in a sharp breath as you understand now that Jesus will be fulfilling a prophecy. He is to enter in peace the city whose name means "City of Peace." Moving quickly now with excitement, you and other disciples spread your cloaks on the donkey's back as a makeshift saddle, and you kneel down on one knee to help Jesus mount. He places his left foot on your thigh, swings his right leg over the donkey's back, adjusts himself momentarily, and then turns to you with a nod. You take the donkey's lead rope, give a gentle tug, and guide the beast forward. It is late afternoon, and the sun is dipping toward the horizon. Jerusalem is only two miles away, but the donkey plods slowly. On foot, Jesus could certainly travel faster. But you know that Jesus rides the colt not to speed up his journey but to make a statement.

The road to the holy city is choked with seemingly endless crowds of pilgrims. Some sing psalms, and the atmosphere is festive. Upon seeing Jesus, many cry out with joy: "Peace in heaven and glory in the highest!" But while peace in heaven may be on their minds, it is peace on earth that is Jesus' concern. As your entourage descends the Mount of Olives, the city comes into plain sight. Jerusalem: the City of Peace fortified by walls and filled with armed soldiers. As Jesus contemplates the view, he begins to weep; he knows that Jerusalem has had a violent and bloody past, and he knows that it will also have a violent and bloody future. As tears stream down his cheeks, he shares with you and those around you why his heart is breaking: the day will soon come when Jerusalem will be crushed and her people suffer terribly. "If this day you only knew what makes for peace," he lamented with a crack in his voice, "but now it is hidden from your eyes."

Jesus' words scare you and fill you with shame. He longs for his followers to be peacemakers, and you know that, for much of your life, you have wanted to be anything but that. Part of you still struggles to understand why Jesus hasn't used his power to wipe out his enemies. In fact, just days before, that's precisely what you had hoped he would do. You were passing through Samaria, whose people and the Jews had harbored a centuries-old mistrust and animosity. Jesus was well aware of this history, which is why he sent you and another disciple ahead to prepare his way in one Samaritan town. Upon arrival, you sensed the villagers' hostility. There were glares, cold shoulders, and a tone of contempt in their speech. When Jesus himself appeared, the reception was no different. Your stay was short, and when you left, James and John expressed the feelings of everyone in the group. "Lord," they insisted, "do you want us to call down fire from heaven to consume them?" It was for good reason that Jesus had named them "Sons of Thunder," you thought, as you nodded your head in agreement. Those contemptuous Samaritans needed to be taught a lesson.

But Jesus would hear nothing of it. He rebuked the Sons of Thunder, and you hung your head in embarrassment and confusion. Once again, Jesus' intentions had been completely misread. But just then, a memory sprang to mind of Jesus on a grassy hillside, surrounded by thousands who strained to hear every word of his revolutionary teachings: "Love your enemies." "Pray for those who persecute you." "Do good to those who hate you." "Be merciful." And most memorably: "Blessed are the peacemakers, for they will be called children of God." It was then that you understood: Jesus wanted you to be a peacemaker just as he was a peacemaker. Which is why he now sits on the donkey you guide so painfully slowly as admiring crowds pave his way with palm branches and cloaks.

Evidently, you have a great deal to learn about peacemaking. This is apparent the following day, when you, Jesus, and the rest of the disciples enter the great, gilded Temple at Jerusalem's heart, which is filled wall-to-wall with fellow pilgrims. With few exceptions, they are very poor—just like Jesus and his own family. As he passes among them, you can sense his compassion for their sufferings. But then something changes. Jesus stiffens; his muscles tense, and his face looks indignant. He sees moneychangers charging outrageous exchange rates so the impoverished pilgrims can make their offerings with coins not bearing the idolatrous image of the Roman emperor and vendors hawking grossly overpriced lambs and doves for sacrifice that the destitute faithful can scarcely afford but have to purchase in order to fulfill their religious duties. Jesus is livid that such greedy extortion takes place in his Father's house of prayer. Others might have turned a blind eye or shrugged their shoulders with indifference, but Jesus makes a prophetic gesture: he overturns the money-changers' tables and drives out the merchants with a whip of cords. Being a peacemaker, Jesus reveals, sometimes requires taking a stand for justice, especially on behalf of those who can't take a stand for themselves, as justice and peace go hand-in-hand.

Peacemaking, you learn this day, can include defending the rights of others and even defending one's self. But peacemaking never involves retaliation. Jesus demonstrates this principle the following evening, on the very feast of Passover you have come to Jerusalem to celebrate. At the Passover meal itself, Jesus shatters convention and stuns you in the process by taking the traditional unleavened bread and proclaiming, "This is my body, which will be given for you." Next, he identifies his cup of wine as his "blood," which will be "shed for many." To your shock, he has established for you a memorial ritual to remember his upcoming, violent death. It is clear that Jesus wants his death—and the manner of his dying—always to be remembered. But it is also clear that he doesn't wish for it to be avenged. What he wishes instead for his friends that night is *shalom*: the blessing and the gift of peace. "Peace I leave with you," he promises. "My peace I give to you."

Nevertheless, some of you try to avenge Jesus later that same night. Supper is over, and Jesus has led you and your companions to Gethsemane, an olive grove just outside the city walls. All of you know that it is a favorite spot of Jesus'—including Judas, who deserted your group earlier in the evening. He returns while you are at Gethsemane, but he isn't alone: a cohort of Temple guards, armed to the teeth, stands behind him, intending to arrest Jesus—with force, if necessary. In an instant, fear combines with instinct and rage. "Lord," you shout as you glower at Judas, "shall we strike with a sword?"

Peter, your fellow apostle, doesn't wait for an answer. He draws a sword hidden in his cloak and lunges, cutting off the right ear of the arresting mob's closest member: Malchus, a slave of the Jewish High Priest. While Malchus crumples in shock and pain and the guards brace to attack the outnumbered disciples, Jesus shouts a command that stops everyone in their tracks: "Stop, no more of this!" Bending over Malchus, whose eyes are wide with terror as blood pours down his cheek, Jesus gently touches his wound and heals him. Turning then to Peter, he orders him to sheathe his weapon, warning that "all who take the sword will perish by the sword." Next, facing you and the rest of the apostles, he assures you that, if he asked, his Father in heaven would rush legions of angels to his defense right then and there. You desperately wish that he would and, for a fleeting moment, think that he might. But when Jesus consents to be arrested, any remaining courage you have vanishes, and you and your companions flee into the night's darkness.

This is the last time you see Jesus for three days. While you hide in fear, you hear reports of how he has been condemned to death and brutally crucified. You weep with grief and shame as rage builds in your heart. Jesus' death, you determine, cannot go unanswered; it must be avenged. Someone needs to pay a price; justice requires it. Jesus may have forbidden taking an eye for an eye, but that approach has obviously failed. You would honor his memory not by following his teaching but by seeking revenge. Violence must be met with power, not peacemaking. Those who take the sword may indeed perish by the sword, but evidently those who don't live by the sword perish, too. While he lived, Jesus had challenged your zeal for violent revolution. But none of that matters now. He is gone forever.

Except that he isn't. On the third day after his death, Jesus appears to you and your fellow disciples in Jerusalem. As you are speechless with joy, Jesus breaks the silence. He makes no mention of revenge, retaliation, or retribution. Instead, he echoes his words from your meal together on Passover night: "Peace be with you." He says this twice, as if to underscore the importance of his message. As years pass, you will recall this message every time you celebrate the memorial of that Passover meal at what came to be called the "Lord's Supper." The *presbyter*—the leader—will repeat Jesus' words of peace, and then everyone will exchange peace with each other by a kiss. Jesus' violent death will be recalled by his broken body and outpoured blood being shared and consumed as blessed bread and wine. Yet this will be received not with outrage but with thanksgiving and capped by the entire assembly being sent forth into the world, not as avengers of Jesus but as agents of his peace.

Questions
for Journaling, Contemplation, or Conversation

1) In view of your present circumstances and relationships, would you consider yourself a peacemaker? Why do you say that?

2) In your opinion, is peace in our world today a naïve wish or realistic goal? What makes it so?

Stop and Pray

O Jesus,
Amidst a joyful crowd at Passover,
you entered fortified Jerusalem, the "City of Peace,"
as a humble herald of peace.
In our conflicted and violent world, show me today
what makes for peace.
Help me to be merciful and love my enemies,
that I may always be known as a child of God.
Amen.

Going Deeper

Mark 11:1–11	Jesus' Entry into Jerusalem
Luke 10:4	Jesus and Companions Travelled Lightly
Luke 6:15	Simon Identified as a Zealot
Matthew 21:4–5 Zechariah 9:9	Why Jesus Entered Jerusalem on a Donkey
Psalm 120–134	Psalms Sung by Pilgrims to Jerusalem
Luke 19:41–44	Jesus Weeps Over Jerusalem
Luke 9:51–55	Samaritan Town Rejects Jesus

Matthew 5:1, 10, 38–48	Peacemaking and Love of Enemies
Mark 11:15–19	Cleansing of the Temple
Matthew 26:28	Jesus' Body and Blood Given for Others
John 14:27	Gift of Peace Given at Last Supper
Matthew 26:31–56 Luke 22:47–51 John 18:1–11	Jesus Consents to Arrest without Violence
John 20:19–23	The Risen Jesus Greets His Disciples

10. THOMAS

REAL PRESENCE

Who was St. Thomas?

St. Thomas became known as "doubting Thomas" because he initially refused to accept that Jesus had risen. Unless he could see and touch Jesus, Thomas protested, "I will not believe." When Jesus later presented himself, Thomas exclaimed, "My Lord and my God!" In response, Jesus insisted, "Blessed are those who have not seen and have believed."

Scripture recalls two other occasions when Thomas spoke. When Jesus set forth toward certain danger in Judea, Thomas said to his fellow apostles, "Let us also go to die with him." And when Jesus shared that he was leaving to prepare a heavenly home for his followers, Thomas asked, "Master, we do not know where you are going; how can we know the way?" While he might not have been willing to believe in Jesus' resurrection without proof, Thomas willingly followed Jesus wherever he led, and after the Resurrection, tradition says that Thomas took the Gospel to India, where he is revered to this day.

• • • • •

While ascending the hill leading to the tiny village of Nain, the Plain of Jezreel unfolds before you, lush with fields of wheat and barley. Two miles distant, Mount Tabor stands sentinel in solitary glory; beyond, the white tipped peak of Mount Hermon glistens in the sunlight. As you continue climbing, your heart begins to pound; you pause not just to catch your breath but to also admire the beautiful expanse of God's creation that greets you. A treasured verse from the scriptures springs to mind: "O Lord, our Lord, how awesome is your name through all the earth! I will sing of your majesty above the heavens."

What you encounter in the village, however, shatters your reverie. At the humble entrance, flanked by the simple mud houses typical of Galilee, a weathered woman in a widow's rough sackcloth, her head covered with ashes and dust, holds her face in her hands as she sobs uncontrollably and slowly labors forward. Following are neighbors and next-of-kin; some of them have torn their clothes to express their grief. Men beat their breasts, and women wail out loud and clap in rhythm as the procession creeps toward the burial caves farther up the hill. As is customary, two flutists, hired for the occasion, play a dirge. Wrapped in a shroud with a handkerchief covering his face and laid upon a bier shouldered by the stronger men is the reason for this sorrowful procession: the body of one of their own who has died only the day before.

Voices are audible over the lamenting flutes as you, Jesus, and your fellow apostles approach ever more closely. Keeping with tradition, the voices loudly extol the virtues of the deceased. From what you hear, you quickly piece together that the person being mourned was a young man, cut down by illness in the prime of his life. That is tragedy enough to grip your heart with sorrow. But when you learn that he was the only son of his widowed mother, your heart is broken. Without a husband or son to support her, she has lost claim to any property or land her family may have owned and become completely dependent on relatives and neighbors. Alone and poor, she is truly to be pitied.

Glancing sideways at Jesus, you can tell that his heart is shattered as well. Countless times you have witnessed his compassion for the sick, the hungry, the forgotten, and those cast to the fringes of society by their difficult circumstances or bad choices. But he seems to have a particular concern for widowed mothers. His own mother, Mary, is a widow, and he has seen the pain she suffered when her beloved Joseph died and knows the strain this loss placed upon her as she continued to raise him, her only son, into adulthood. You aren't shocked, then, when Jesus, having surmised the gravity of the situation, approaches the weeping widow with an expression mixed of both affection and concern.

What does shock you is what happens next. You expect that Jesus will offer words of comfort and perhaps give her a blessing. But when he says, "Do not weep," you are taken aback. It is obvious to all why she is weeping: her only son had just died. How can Jesus, whose thoughts and words always seem to penetrate human hearts, be so oblivious and insensitive? For a fleeting moment, you think of pulling him aside and trying to salvage the situation, as you can see confusion and anger on the villagers' faces. Jesus is faster than you, however. He approaches the bier, grips the corpse, and in an assertive tone orders, "Young man, I tell you, arise!"

Never mind that, according to Jewish law, touching a dead body renders a person ritually unclean, unable to participate in the community's worship. Because moments after Jesus issues his command, the body stirs and begins to wrestle free of the burial wrappings. The bier is quickly lowered, and a ruddy, bearded face emerges from under the cloth that had concealed it.

He appears bewildered, as does everyone else. For a long moment, the entire assembly stands motionless, in stunned silence. Then pandemonium breaks loose. The young man jumps up and embraces his mother while both shed rivers of tears. Meanwhile, the onlookers cry aloud that a great prophet is in their midst and, memorably, "God has visited his people!" You have to agree: the dead has just been raised.

For many of the townsfolk, this miracle brings to mind a remarkable incident that took place in the neighboring village of Shunem. After a woman there lost her only son, God restored him to life through the prophet Elisha. This story was cherished, but it had taken place a good eight hundred years before. In your day, people are longing for God to show his powerful and loving hand again, but he has seemed to be absent. Your ancestors had believed God to be present and active in the life of his people. "For what great nation is there," asked Moses, "that has gods so close to it as the Lord, our God, is to us whenever we call upon him?" While it is still understood that God dwells in the Jerusalem Temple behind a great curtain in the Holy of Holies, only the high priest can presume to enter there, and even he can do so just once a year. Any other person who dares to enter, it is warned, will be struck dead. God now seems inaccessible and fearsome; that's why people hunger for him to again be with them and to speak and act in their midst. You share this hope. That's why you have become a follower of Jesus.

After witnessing Jesus raise the dead, you are convinced that God has visited his people again. You conclude that Jesus must surely be the Messiah, God's longed-for anointed one who will save your people and make them a great nation again. So when Jesus informs you and your fellow disciples that you will travel to Bethany so he can attend to his sick friend Lazarus, nothing can possibly deter you from accompanying him. Danger likely awaits you there, as Jesus' ministry has aroused hostility among the religious authorities in nearby Jerusalem. But while you are not without fear, you are committed and determined. To your hesitant companions, you said, "Let us also go to die with him."

When you arrive at Bethany, Lazarus has already died, and Jesus weeps openly. Then he orders the stone sealing Lazarus's tomb to be removed. Onlookers protest, insisting that there will be a stench. But you smile to yourself, as you know what Jesus will do next. Jesus bellows for his friend to come out, and Lazarus shambles forth, struggling to be liberated from his burial shroud. Those who witness this are just as taken aback as those at Nain had been, and they, too, cry out in amazement. You share their joy but not their shock, as you have seen Jesus restore life to the dead before. God is continuing to visit his people, and you feel confident, secure, and unafraid.

Your courage evaporates in a matter of days. Jesus enters Jerusalem, and in a borrowed upper room, he celebrates the Passover supper along with all the disciples. Breaking convention, he takes bread, blesses it, breaks it, and explains that it is his body that will be given up for you; then he shares it with everyone to eat. He next takes his cup of wine, says that it is his blood which will be shed for the forgiveness of sins, and passes it around for everyone to drink. This puzzles and distresses you, as does much of what Jesus says that evening. "I will be with you only a little while longer," he promises. "Where I go you cannot come." You are crestfallen! For three years you have been with him, following him into the teeth of danger, even to the point of risking death. And now he is going away—and leaving you behind. "Where I am going, you know the way," Jesus continued. Except that you don't. Speaking for all your companions, you insist, "Master, we do not know where you are going; how can we know the way?" Looking intently at you,

Jesus answers, "I am the way, the truth, and the life."
But in your sorrow and confusion, those words mean
nothing to you. All you know is that in Jesus, God has
visited his people. And now he is going away.

Jesus does go away—that very night. He is taken
away, to be more precise. After the Passover meal, Jesus
leads you and the rest of the disciples to Gethsemane, a
garden just outside the city gates, where he is arrested.
As he is led away under armed escort, you flee into
the darkness. The following day, Jesus is crucified. You
aren't there to witness it, but you hear reports from
those who were. You are numb with shock and grief.
Jesus had raised the dead! How can he himself be dead?
Why didn't he save himself? Your head hurts, and your
heart aches. God is with his people no longer. He is gone
because Jesus is gone. You are confused. But most of all,
you feel angry. Angry at those who killed Jesus. Angry
at Jesus for not having stopped them.

On the third day after Jesus has died, your companions report that Jesus is alive again, but you can't
believe your ears. You are convinced that he is gone. He
had said he was going away and that none of you could
follow. And now he's come back? Your friends plead
for you to believe them until they are blue in the face,
insisting over and over that they have been with Jesus
himself and that he has visited them in person. But you
think they must be delusional or have seen a strange
vision. "Unless I put my finger into the nailmarks, and
put my hand into his side," you stubbornly refuse, "I
will not believe."

Seven days later, you have your chance. You are
with your companions on the evening of the first day
of the week—just as the rest of them had been together
the week before. And once again, Jesus appears. It isn't
a vision or a hallucination. He is there in the flesh, and
he eats a fish as if to prove that he isn't a ghost. Then
he directs his gaze toward you, not in reproach or

disappointment but with understanding and, as always, compassion. He holds out his hand and invites you to touch. "Put your finger here and see my hands, and bring your hand and put it into my side, and do not be unbelieving, but believe." Then he says further, "Blessed are those who have not seen and have believed." You decline Jesus' invitation to touch him. There is no need; you already believe. Falling to your knees, you exclaim in astonishment, "My Lord and my God." In a moment of insight, you recognize that God didn't simply visit his people through Jesus as he had with prophets like Elisha. Instead, Jesus is God himself, walking among his people. He is the very Son of God.

Jesus does leave you again. It is this departure he had referred to at the Passover meal with words that left you so perplexed. As you and your friends watch him ascend into heaven, Jesus promises, "Behold, I am with you always, even to the end of the age." Comforting words, but again you feel confused. With him gone, how can he possibly keep his promise? How can he be in heaven and with his people on earth at the same time? You continue to be puzzled until you gather with your companions to celebrate the Lord's Supper, as Jesus had commanded you to do at that final Passover meal. During the supper, Jesus' words are repeated over bread and wine: "This is my body." "This is my blood." It dawns on you: Jesus is there, in his flesh and blood. God is truly present to his people. It doesn't look as if he is; he doesn't appear to be present, but you know him to be. Believing without seeing is no longer a problem for you, and that is a blessing. As Jesus himself said, "Blessed are those who have not seen and have believed."

Questions
for Journaling, Contemplation, or Conversation

1) Do you find it difficult to have faith? Do you struggle with doubts? Why or why not?

2) Do you find God to be present and active in your life or remote and absent?

Stop and Pray

My Lord and my God,
You said that they are blessed who have not seen
and yet believe.
Yet while you are so close to me,
I sometimes doubt your presence
and refuse to believe unless I touch and see.
Strengthen my faith that you are with me always
as the way, the truth, and the life.
Amen.

Going Deeper

Psalm 8:2	Psalm in Praise of God's Creation
Luke 7:11–17	Widow's Son Restored to Life
Numbers 19:11	Touching a Dead Body Renders One Unclean
2 Kings 4:8–37	Elisha and the Woman of Shunem
Deuteronomy 4:7	Moses Speaks of God's Closeness to His People
Hebrews 9:7	High Priest Enters Temple Once Yearly
John 11:1–44	Lazarus Raised by Jesus at Bethany

Matthew 26:26–30	The Last Supper
John 14:1–14	Jesus Explains that He Is Going Away
Mark 14:32–15:47	Arrest and Crucifixion of Jesus
John 20:24–29	Thomas Doubts Reports of the Resurrection
Matthew 28:20	Jesus Promises to Remain with His Followers

11. PHILIP

service to the poor

Who was St. Philip?

St. Philip was from Bethsaida, along with Andrew and Peter. Jesus called Philip to become an apostle with a simple invitation: "Follow me." Philip then found Nathanael, also known as Bartholomew, and insisted he "come and see" Jesus. Although he was a Jew from Galilee, Philip's name was Greek, and he was once approached by certain Greeks for an introduction to Jesus. When facing a hungry crowd in the wilderness, Jesus asked Philip how to get food for them. In response, Philip declared that "two hundred days' wages worth of food would not be enough for each of them to have a little." After this, Jesus fed the crowd by multiplying a handful of loaves and fishes. It is said that after the Resurrection, Philip preached the Gospel in Greece, Syria, and Phrygia, along with his sister Mariamne and Bartholomew.

• • • • • •

It is a deserted area, a fair hike from tiny Bethsaida, your hometown along the shores of the Sea of Galilee. Not a single sign of human habitation meets your eyes as you survey the surrounding landscape, but you aren't lost. In fact, you know this country quite well, having wandered here often since you were a boy, sometimes with Andrew, your lifelong friend. Jesus has become familiar with this area, too, but he relies on your knowledge of the byways and footpaths, some used only by lonely shepherds and their flocks. Nearby Capernaum has been a base for his ministry, and it was near there where you were first introduced to Jesus, who called you to be his disciple with the simple invitation, "Follow me." You accepted, as you had begun to wonder if perhaps he might be the Messiah, the longed-for savior of your people, the Jews. At the very least, you were certain that he was a mighty prophet, through whom God was doing great things.

Today, Jesus is mourning the death of another prophet, John the Baptist—his kinsman who had prepared his way by preaching repentance and baptizing followers in the shallow, murky waters of the Jordan River. As prophets do, John had spoken truth to power, and the power he challenged reacted by first arresting him and then murdering him in prison. His blood was on the hands of Herod, the local puppet ruler and conspirator with the hated Romans, who tolerated him for expediency's sake but could remove him in a heartbeat if they wished. Herod was acutely aware of this, and his contempt and fear made him paranoid and tyrannical. John the Baptist was simply the latest victim of his cruelty, of which there were too many to count. He'd been beheaded upon Herod's orders, the tragic conclusion of an arrogant, drunken promise made to impress party guests.

Jesus has taken the news of his relative's death hard, and its impact upon him is evident. His eyes have a faraway look, he speaks very little, and the expression on his face is a mixture of both pain and concern. All life is precious to Jesus—that has been clear from the moment you began to follow him—and he invariably shows compassion to the dying or those who have just lost a loved one. John's death, however, is deeply personal for Jesus. Not only was it exceptionally senseless and cruel but he and John shared blood ties, and their mothers had been very close. As you watch him, you wonder if Jesus fears that John's grisly fate might one day be his as well. Like John, Jesus also speaks truth to power. And power has begun to notice.

In fact, many people notice what Jesus says and does—not just the handful of those who wield power but especially the masses who do not. Enthusiastic crowds greet him almost everywhere he goes. This is a blessing, but it can also be exhausting as they bring with them great needs and sometimes insistent demands. Jesus often has to speak outdoors, as no house or synagogue can accommodate those who seek his words of wisdom or healing touch. When traveling from town to town, bodies press upon his entourage, mothers impose children upon him to bless, and necks strain to catch a glimpse or hear his teaching over the din of voices, occasionally punctuated by shouts of praise. Yet in spite of the chaos, Jesus loves all who come to him—even those with hostile intent. He can't seem to do anything else.

Sometimes, however, Jesus needs to escape from the crowds—to be alone with you and your fellow disciples to teach, talk, and share a leisurely meal. Occasionally, he leaves your group altogether and spends a night on a mountain in solitude, praying with his Father. After hearing the devastating news of John's execution, he expresses a wish to get away, and you suggest the deserted place that you found yourself this day. Surely, you conclude, this is a secluded-enough spot where Jesus can rest and grieve. Jesus' admirers might be passionate, you reason, but they won't follow him to this remote location, far from their homes. Or so you think. But you've underestimated their enthusiasm for Jesus and the hope his ministry engenders.

When you arrive at what you'd hoped would be a peaceful place, you are surprised that a crowd has already assembled there. You haven't a clue as to how they knew where to find Jesus, but their numbers continue to grow until thousands have gathered, waiting for Jesus to speak, waiting for anything to happen. Initially, you think that Jesus might dismiss them and continue further into the wilderness. But when he surveys their faces, the grief that has been so evident on his own face since John's death is replaced with compassion. He sees their needs, and in his love for them, he is not going to turn anyone away. And so he begins to speak to them about love, mercy, and the kingdom of God. They don't tire of listening, and Jesus does not appear to tire of speaking.

The day wears on, and still Jesus continues. As the sun dips toward the horizon, you begin to worry. From what you can see, no one in the crowd has any food with them. Perhaps they'd brought some when they set out from their homes, but whatever they once had is now long gone. You know that they are hungry because most of them are always hungry. A fair number appear weak and gaunt on account of malnutrition. The majority are farmers, and few have sufficient land to grow enough food to feed their families, let alone satisfy Herod's increasing taxes. Those taxes have forced some to sell their lands to pay their debts, and they've found themselves toiling for others on land that had once been their own. Some have turned to fishing, but unless they have access to expensive boats and tackle, fishing from the shore seldom meets with success. Others have become laborers, working for meager wages to build new cities financed by the very taxes that have forced them to leave their former livelihoods.

It is a cruel system, and Jesus is no stranger to it. He himself had grown up poor; he is the son of a carpenter, Joseph, whose distant ancestor was the great Jewish king David but whose more recent ancestor had lost his family's land, forcing him to leave farming. Thankfully, Joseph usually had steady work and had been able to pass on his skills to Jesus. But he had been poor, nevertheless. Shortly after Jesus was born, he and his wife Mary presented their child in the Jerusalem Temple, as custom required. There they made an offering of two turtledoves—the offering prescribed for those too poor to afford a sheep or a goat. During his ministry, Jesus taught often about God's special love for the poor and that those with more have a sacred responsibility to share with those who have less. And while Jesus would sometimes dine with the rich as a guest in their homes, some of his sharpest criticisms were directed at the greed and indifference he would encounter among them. Jesus himself lived simply, and he expected his disciples to do the same.

As the sun continues to set, its lengthening rays sparkle on the waters of the Sea of Galilee, which are especially calm and peaceful today. While you survey the crowd, still attentive to Jesus, your stomach growls with hunger, and you are sure that yours isn't the only one. Your group has no provisions to share with so many, although you desperately wish that you did. Someone suggests that Jesus send the crowd away to buy something to eat in the neighboring towns—assuming, of course, that they have money in their belts, which they very well may not. But what happens next is a complete surprise. Jesus turns directly to you and asks, "Where can we buy enough food for them to eat?" You are incredulous. How can Jesus expect you and your companions to live simply and yet have the resources on hand to feed such a vast crowd?

"Lord," you plead, "two hundred days' wages worth of food would not be enough for each of them to have a little." Just then, Andrew appears with a little boy who has been generous enough to share his two small fish and five loaves of barley bread—the staple food of the poor. "Daily bread," it is called. But while he is touched by the boy's gesture, Andrew states the obvious: his gift of so little is of no benefit for so many.

Jesus appears unconcerned, however, and seems to know exactly what to do. He orders everyone to recline on the nearby grass, which is abundant, lush, and green, as it is springtime. Then he takes the bread, says the traditional Jewish blessing of thanksgiving, breaks the loaves, and gives them to you and your fellow disciples to distribute to the crowds. You do so in obedience but also with confusion, as the morsels you begin to place in the crowd's eager, grasping hands are sure to be gone quickly. But then, to your astonishment, you realize that the bread isn't running out at all. Instead, it is multiplying, so everyone has enough to eat. In fact, they have more than enough to eat, and after everyone is full, twelve baskets of leftovers are gathered up. Five small loaves have fed more than five thousand mouths.

As this miracle unfolds before your eyes and you witness the joy on the faces of those savoring what for them is a banquet, a passage from the scriptures comes to mind, as it seems to describe what Jesus has just done. "The Lord is my shepherd," it begins, "there is nothing I lack." Jesus, you recalled, had once noted that the crowds seemed like sheep without a shepherd; by providing them with nourishment they'd needed, he had made himself their shepherd. Today, Jesus had ordered the crowds to recline in the grass next to the calmed sea. This recalls the scripture passage, too. "In green pastures he makes me lie down," it continues, "to still waters he leads me." It goes on to say, "You set a table before me. . . . You anoint my head with oil." This is a reference to a feast, and you have just witnessed Jesus feed the people he loves with an abundance they have never before seen. You smile as you reflect on all this, as you are now able to appreciate Jesus in a way you haven't before: as a gentle shepherd who tends to the needs of his flock.

The crowds, however, understand him differently. In their excitement and gratitude, they want to make him their king. While Jesus has just shown them that he is their shepherd, what they want instead is a ruler—a powerful one. In particular, they want a ruler who will lead them in overthrowing their present rulers, who are oppressing them terribly. But that isn't Jesus' plan. That's why, before things get out of hand, he escapes into the night, where he is finally able to enjoy a little of the solitude for which he longs. By the next day, however, the crowds have caught up with him again. They have encountered someone who has given them hope, and they want to hear and see more. And just as much, they are hungry again and eager for more food. Jesus knows this full well. So this time, instead of feeding them, he teaches them and challenges them. He wants the crowd to understand who he really is and what he is about.

The day before, the crowd had been with Jesus in the wilderness. Today, Jesus reminds the crowd of another wilderness: the wilderness in which their ancestors had wandered for an entire generation as they'd made their way from slavery in Egypt to a new homeland God had promised them. Like the crowd with Jesus, that ancient crowd had been hungry, too. And God had fed them— not with barley bread but with manna: a fine, flake-like food that was gathered off the ground each morning. Unlike the barley bread, however, there was only just enough manna each day for people to eat what they needed. There was no surplus, in contrast to the bushels of leftovers you had helped gather up. This abundance of barley bread suggested that it was a gift far greater than that of the manna, which is precisely the point Jesus stresses when he speaks. "Your ancestors ate the manna in the desert, but they died," he begins. That is true enough. But what he says next is not only

unexpected, it is downright breathtaking: "I am the living bread that came down from heaven. Whoever eats
this bread will live forever."

Every Jew in that crowd knows that manna had
been God's gift from heaven. But they also know that
the manna simply nourished; it didn't give everlasting
life. Yet Jesus just said that he gives a bread which offers
precisely that. Some in the crowd are scandalized and
march off indignantly. Others stay but are understand-
ably confused. You are among them. What kind of bread
is Jesus talking about? The barley bread from the day
before? To you, its multiplication had been a miracle that
was a sign of Jesus' compassion for the hungry poor,
whom he fed as a shepherd cares for his sheep. That you
understand. But could the barley bread also have been
a sign of something else? Did it somehow point to the
bread of life of which Jesus speaks? Perhaps. But for the
time being, all you can do is wonder.

The mystery is solved at Passover. You, Jesus, and
the other disciples are in Jerusalem to celebrate that
feast at which every Jew commemorates God's having
liberated their ancestors from Egyptian slavery centuries before. In a large upper room, everyone reclines on
cushions as is customary. Being in that position, your
mind flashes back to that day when Jesus instructed the
hungry crowds to recline on the green grass. Later, when
Jesus takes the traditional unleavened bread and blesses
it, breaks it, and gives it to everyone to eat, you remember that same day again, as Jesus had done the very
same thing with the barley loaves from the little boy.
Moments later, when Jesus calls the unleavened bread
his "body," you recall his words to the crowd when he
insisted that his "body," the "bread of life," is the only
food which gives eternal life. It then becomes clear to
you: while the barley bread Jesus fed his hungry sheep
was greater that the ancient gift of manna, it also held a
key to understanding the "bread of life" Jesus gives to

his disciples this Passover night. While the barley loaves pointed forward to the bread of life, the bread of life hearkens back to the barley loaves and Jesus' compassion for the hungry crowd. In other words, Jesus wants those who receive his bread of life to imitate his loving care for the poor.

Jesus soon dies, rises, and ascends to heaven. After this, you and the other disciples begin to preach Jesus' good news far and wide. As a boy, you and Andrew had hiked the remote paths beyond Bethsaida on which you later led Jesus to where he fed his hungry sheep. Now, you travel not with Andrew but with Bartholomew and Mariamne, your sister. These journeys take you much farther from home: to Greece, Phrygia, and Syria. But regardless of where you go, you encounter the impoverished, the famished, the oppressed. And, having been nourished by Jesus' bread of life, you do whatever you can to nourish his hungry sheep. Just like a shepherd. Just like Jesus himself.

Questions
for Journaling, Contemplation, or Conversation

1) What prophetic figures have inspired you? Why do you admire them?

2) Does your faith impact your response to hunger and need in your community?

Stop and Pray

Good Shepherd,
In compassion for the needs of your flock,
you set a table before me
and lead me to green pastures beside still waters.
Fill me with your compassion

as you sustain me with living bread.
Teach me to imitate your loving concern
for the hungry and poor.
Amen.

Going Deeper

John 1:43–51	Philip Introduced to Jesus
Matthew 14:1–13	John the Baptist's Death and Jesus' Grief
Luke 1:39–45	Closeness between Jesus' and John's Mothers
Mark 2:2; 3:20; 4:1; 10:13–16	Crowds Press upon Jesus
Mark 6:30–33	Crowds Follow Jesus into the Wilderness
Mark 6:34	Jesus Teaches the Hungry Crowds
Luke 2:24	Offering of the Poor Made by Jesus' Family
Leviticus 5:7	
Luke 1:53; 4:18; 6:20; 7:22;	God's Love for the Poor
Matthew 19:23–26 Luke 6:24; 14:13; 16:20–22; 18:18–23; 19:1–10	Responsibility to the Poor
Psalm 23	The Good Shepherd Feeds His People
John 6:14	Crowds Seek to Make Jesus King
Luke 14	Jesus Dines with the Rich
Mark 6:35–44; John 6:1–13	Hungry Crowd Fed with Loaves and Fishes
John 6:22–51	Jesus Teaches About Bread from Heaven
Exodus 16	God Feeds the Israelites with Manna
John 6:60–66	Disciples Leave Jesus over His Teachings
Luke 22:14–20	Jesus Offers His Body at the Last Supper
Acts 8	Missionary Journeys of Philip

12. Andrew

work

Who was St. Andrew?

Along with his older brother Peter, St. Andrew was a fisherman of the Sea of Galilee, as was Jonas, their father. Although Andrew was raised in Bethsaida, as an adult he shared a home with Peter in Capernaum, where they engaged in a cooperative fishing enterprise with James and John. At one time, Andrew may have been a follower of John the Baptist, but he became the first to be called as a disciple of Jesus, who promised that he would become a "fisher of men." As a disciple, scripture recalls that Andrew presented to Jesus a boy "with five barley loaves and two fish." Andrew asked, "What good are these for so many?" but Jesus multiplied them to feed a crowd of thousands. After the Resurrection, traditions recall Andrew taking the Gospel to modern-day Turkey.

• • • • • •

As the first glimmers of sunrise appear on the horizon, your heart sinks, as it signals the end of another fruitless night of fishing. Your muscles are cramped and aching from the hard labor of casting nets, pulling oars, and manning the sails of your heavy oak and cedar craft which, if necessary, can carry fifteen people. Your name, Andrew, means "manly" or "brave," but you certainly don't feel that way now. With exhaustion, frustration, and hunger, you slump over in the rounded stern and gaze into the still darkness of the waters off the port side. As your stomach growls, you anxiously twist the end of your beard with heavily calloused fingers; no catch means no income for today. Sure, there have always been mornings as a fisherman when you've rowed back to shore with empty nets; in the past, they didn't concern you all that much, as the following night would almost invariably bring better luck. However, nights of empty nets now seem to happen much more frequently. And you feel afraid.

Your anxiety has nothing to do with your skill as a fisherman. Along with your older brother, Simon, you grew up in a small fishing village on the shores of the Sea of Galilee, whose depths you had fished since you were a boy. You are intimately familiar with all eighteen types of fish that can be caught in these waters, which you've joked you could navigate blindfolded if necessary. Both you and Simon have been taught well by your father, Jonas, who himself had been a fisherman, as had his father before him. You are a son of a fisherman surrounded by other fishermen; Bethsaida, your hometown's name, actually means "house of a fishermen." Until recently, you couldn't imagine doing another form of work. But now, you have begun to wonder.

New fishermen have recently been arriving at the lake. Unlike you, they did not grow up fishing and typically have rudimentary skills, at best. Most of them had been farmers, working land that their ancestors had owned for generations. Rising taxes had led them into debt, however, forcing them to sell their land and abandon the only way of providing for themselves and their families that they have ever known. Some ended up working as farm laborers on lands they once owned. Others, however, have turned to fishing, hoping for a new livelihood or at least a decent meal. Initially, they tried to fish from the shore, but these efforts produced more frustration than fish. As you know well, success requires a boat with someone experienced enough to guide it to the most abundant fishing grounds, at times through dangerous, storm-tossed waters. That's why some of the desperate new arrivals pool their meager resources and hire boats with seasoned mariners. The lake has become crowded with fishermen, the fish population has sunk, and an increasing number of boats, like yours, return home at sunrise with empty nets.

At times, you and Simon wonder out loud what can be done. There are plenty of opportunities to speak about this dilemma. Not only do you work together but you are presently living with Simon, his wife, and her mother. Nevertheless, the two of you have yet to come up with any viable solutions. Other established fishermen want to drive off the new competitors, but neither of you support this approach. In spite of the threat they pose to your business, you have compassion for their plight, as their suffering is real. They had arrived frightened and hungry, and they are desperate to provide for their wives and children. Had you walked in their sandals, you would be doing exactly the same thing. Nevertheless, your sympathy for their situation doesn't suggest any alternative sources of revenue for you and Peter. Fishing is the only way of life either of you have ever known, and you have few other practical skills. In your heart of hearts, you will be a fisherman for life, and you know it.

This particular morning, there is nothing more to do than haul your boat ashore, wash your nets, and pray that the next night will bring an abundant catch. As you approach land, you notice that a crowd has assembled. This is unusual; usually the shore is empty at this time of day except for a few other fishermen or merchants who had come to inspect what they have caught. But as you row closer, you can see why there is a gathering:

Jesus of Nazareth is preaching. Recently, he has attracted quite a following by healing the sick and teaching about what he calls the "kingdom of God." He had even cured Peter's mother-in-law of a severe fever in the very home you share, and you know that John, the baptizer and a prophet you greatly admire, had been awaiting his arrival. Jesus speaks of love and mercy, and his message falls on receptive ears among the suffering and desperate. The entire community is buzzing with excitement about him, and you hope that, while your nets are drying, you might have an opportunity to hear what he has to say.

You pull up near the crowd, disembark, and begin to wash your nets with Simon. Another boat pulls up alongside. It, too, is manned by a pair of brothers: James and John, who are business partners with you and Simon; together, you've pooled resources to afford your boats and other equipment, and the arrangement has worked well. As the four of you work, the crowd takes little notice of you, but Jesus certainly does. He recognizes you and Simon and sees your boat as an opportunity to gain a little distance from the crowd, which has been pressing upon him. With your enthusiastic consent, Jesus climbs on board, sits down on the stern, and begins to teach. You are excited and humbled to have such a distinguished guest on your vessel, and you forget all about your lack of fish. Jesus doesn't, however. When he has finished teaching, he instructs Simon to row to deeper waters. Simon protests: "We have worked hard all night and have caught nothing!" Jesus is a carpenter by trade; you wonder what he knows about fishing, if anything. Simon surely wonders the same thing. Nevertheless, you are aware that Jesus has done some remarkable things and that everything he says carries a great weight of authority—including his instruction to cast your nets one more time. Which Simon does.

As the sun is already high in the sky, your chances of catching anything are slim. But in obedience to the one who had healed his mother-in-law, Simon lowers his net into the water. Within minutes it is swelling with fish, and Simon alone can't haul it in. You rush to help, but even the two of you find it impossible to lift this bounty into the boat. In fact, your nets are threatening to tear, and you fear losing the entire catch. Jesus joins the effort but to no avail. Meanwhile, James and John have been watching in astonishment off your starboard bow. Frantically, you yell and gesture for them to help, and moments later, they row up alongside. With ten arms now working in unison, you pull in the nets, just as they are about to burst. Even so, your struggle isn't over. Under the colossal weight of the fish, flopping and floundering in a teeming mass under the rising mid-morning sun, your boat's wooden hull planks creak in protest, and the waterline dips perilously low. For a brief moment, you have a fleeting vision of a sinking craft, a desperate swim back to shore, and certain financial ruin. Simon is fearful, too, and falls on his knees before Jesus, begging him to leave. But Jesus simply smiles and speaks reassuring words. "Do not be afraid," he says, "from now on you will be catching men."

From this day forward, you leave everything behind and follow Jesus. You are still a fisherman and always will be. But now, instead of trolling the waters of the Sea of Galilee for fish, you will traverse the towns and countryside of Galilee and beyond, seeking new followers for Jesus. Nets and hooks are no longer your stock-in-trade but the good news of God's kingdom that Jesus has come to proclaim. The nature of your work has changed dramatically and irreversibly. To be sure, from time to time you will return to the open water. After Jesus dies, in your confusion about what to do next, you will resume fishing, as it will be familiar and even comforting—not to mention a source of income.

Nevertheless, you are now, first and foremost, a disciple. Jesus has called you from your boats to a different way of life.

Yet even as Jesus invites you to embrace a new reality, he still honors your old livelihood by continuing to call you a fisherman—a "fisher of men," to be precise. And you never forget that he's called you to this new line of work within the context of your old one. Jesus has honored your work. In fact, as you come to know him, you see that Jesus honors all honest work. Jesus himself had been a skilled laborer for most of his life, having learned carpentry and stone work from Joseph, his father. Like yours, his work had been physically strenuous and even dangerous at times, and his prospects for income had never been quite certain. He has lived the life that many of those who come to listen to him have lived, and he wants to offer them hope. "Come to me, all you who labor and are burdened," he promises, "and I will give you rest." And when he teaches them, he often makes references to their different forms of labor so they can better understand God's love for them and God's respect and appreciation for what they do.

You like it especially when Jesus speaks of fishing. When he tells a story of fishermen letting down their nets into a lake, catching many types of fish and sorting them along the shore, you smile. And when he references the old wisdom of "red sky at night, sailors' delight; red sky at morning, sailors take warning," you nod in approval. Jesus peppers his preaching with images from many other fields of work as well. He speaks of farmers sowing and reaping, gathering crops into barns, separating wheat from chaff, pulling and burning weeds, and yoking oxen. He is familiar with different conditions of soil and the knowledge that summer is approaching when the twigs on fig trees became tender and leaves appear. Day laborers in a marketplace seeking vineyard work form the basis of one parable, you recall. In fact, Jesus is quite familiar with vineyards and their operations. He tells of storing wine in wineskins, of pruning vines to make them more fruitful, and of vineyards guarded by walls and watchtowers. And once, he makes the obvious point that grapes aren't picked from briers, which brings a chuckle to all who hear.

Sheep and shepherds are familiar to Jesus, too. He knows well the hazardous work of guarding sheep from wolves, rescuing them after they fall into a pit, and searching for strays in the nighttime darkness. Jesus even identifies himself as a shepherd—a "good shepherd"—who, like real shepherds, calls each of his sheep by name when leading them in and out of their pen. Sometimes Jesus alludes to building, his own line of work, when he speaks of laying cornerstones and the importance of placing a foundation on rock instead of sand. When in one story he mentioned a speck of sawdust lodged in one eye, you knew that he'd experienced that many times before. On other occasions, his teaching references students and teachers, household servants and their masters, doctors and bankers, and merchants searching for fine pearls. Jesus is knowledgeable about work done by women, as well: spinning and sewing, patching garments, grinding grain at a mill, kneading dough and baking bread, and caring for children— whom he is always eager to bless.

Jesus' teaching is easy to grasp whenever he presents it through the forms of work people do. He isn't a philosopher from Greece who speaks over people's heads; instead, he has been an ordinary worker like most of his hearers, and this gave him great credibility with them. You can see it whenever you scan faces in the crowds by observing their rapt attention, knowing smiles, and nodding heads. Their hearing that God's kingdom can be understood by how they labor gives them a dignity that is sometimes denied them by others who either lord authority over them or look down upon

them as uneducated or unclean. Every one of Jesus'
Jewish listeners is familiar with the story of Adam and
Eve who, after they were banished from the Garden of
Eden, were consigned to a lifetime of toil, sweat, uncer-
tainty, and frustration. This is typically their experience,
too, just as it is often yours. Instead of being a source of
pride, work seems mostly like punishment. But Jesus is
changing that. Not only does his mentioning their labor
help them understand his message, it also helps them
appreciate their work as noble and good. After all, the
scriptures say that God himself worked when creating
the heavens and the earth and that the fruits of his labors
were "very good." Thanks to Jesus, God's children can
now appreciate their work as "very good," too.

You will often think of this, years later, whenever
you celebrate the Lord's Supper, at which you will
remember how, the night before he died, Jesus blessed
bread and wine, called it his body and blood, and gave
it to his friends to eat and drink. In the prayers of the
Lord's Supper, God will be thanked for the gifts of that
bread and wine. However, those gifts don't arrive fully
formed: the bread begins as grain, which is planted,
harvested, ground into flour, and then oven-baked; the
wine begins as grapes, which are cultivated, crushed,
and fermented in jars. The work of human hands is
required to shape God's good gifts into something else
new and good. At the Lord's Supper, those gifts will
then be offered with gratitude to God, who will bless
them and return them as something even greater: the
body and blood of Jesus. Truly, you will reflect, this is a
wonderful exchange of gifts. But it is one which cannot
happen without the cooperation of God's people and the
hard, noble, and important work they do—whether it be
that of a shepherd, a farmer, a homemaker, a servant, a
fisherman, or a fisher of men.

Questions
for Journaling, Contemplation, or Conversation

1) Have you experienced work more often as a burden or a gift? Why?

2) Has your faith influenced your decisions about work?

Stop and Pray

Jesus, son of a carpenter,
You taught that God's kingdom can be understood
through different forms of work.
In the Eucharist, the offering of my labors
are returned as your Body and Blood.
Through this exchange of gifts, give me gratitude
and strength for my work,
especially when I am exhausted, frustrated, or afraid.
Amen.

Going Deeper

Mark 1:16	Andrew and Simon Peter Are Brothers and Fishermen
John 1:42; 21:17	Jonas Is the Father of Andrew and Peter
John 1:44	Bethsaida the Birthplace of Andrew and Peter
Mark 1:21, 29	Andrew and Peter Share a Capernaum Home
Luke 5:1	Jesus' Preaching Attracts Great Crowds
Mark 1:30–31	Peter's Mother-in-Law Healed by Jesus
John 1:35–40	Andrew a Follower of John the Baptist
Mark 1:16–20; Luke 5:1–11	Jesus Calls Andrew to Be a "Fisher of Men"
Mark 3:13–19	Good News Proclaimed by Andrew

John 21:1–4	Disciples Fishing After the Resurrection
Matthew 13:55 Mark 6:3	Jesus a Carpenter Like Joseph
Matthew 11:28–30	Rest Promised to the Weary
Matthew 13:47–48; 16:1–3 Matthew 3:11–12; 11:29–30; 13:1–9, 18–32; 24:32–35	Fishing Incorporated into Jesus' Teaching
Luke 12:16–21 John 12:24 Matthew 20:1–16 Luke 6:43–45; 20:9–19	Farming References in Jesus' Teaching
John 15:1–9 Matthew 10:16; 12:11–12; 25:31–33; 26:31 Luke 5:36; 15:4–6; 17:7–10	Vineyard Imagery in Jesus' Teaching
John 10:1–18; 21:15–19 Matthew 7:1–5, 24–26; 16:18; 21:42	Sheep and Shepherds in Jesus' Teaching
Matthew 7:1–5 Mark 2:21 Luke 6:46–48	Construction Themes in Jesus' Teaching
Luke 12:23; 13:20–21; 17:35	Women's Work in Jesus' Teaching
Matthew 10:24–25; 13:45–46 Mark 10:13–16 Luke 5:36; 12:35–48; 13:20–21; 14:15–24; 16:1–8	Other Forms of Work Mentioned by Jesus
Genesis 3:17–19	Adam Consigned to Hard Labor
Genesis 1:31; 2:1–3	Fruits of God's Labors Declared "Very Good"
Luke 22:14–20	The Last Supper

13. Mary Magdalene

....

Evangelization

Who was St. Mary Magdalene?

Thanks to her love and courage, St. Mary Magdalene was the first of Jesus' followers to meet the risen Lord, who in turn instructed her to share the good news of the Resurrection with the apostles. For this, she has long been honored as the Proto (First) Evangelist and the Apostle to the Apostles. History has also frequently misunderstood and mislabeled Mary Magdalene, at times insisting that she was a former prostitute or even the wife of Jesus. Scripture suggests, however, that she may have been a financially independent woman whom Jesus healed of an illness. Following her cure, she materially supported Jesus, accompanied him on his missionary journeys, and stood by him as he hung on the cross after all but one of his male disciples had fled in fear.

• • • • • •

Sleep would be a welcome relief, but it never comes. Instead, you spend the night either pacing the floor, frenetic with fear and nervous energy, or sobbing while slumped in a corner, your face buried in your hands. After several hours, the tears no longer flow, your head

119

throbs, and your pacing gives way to a labored slog, as if you are dragging a giant millstone behind you. Brutal images of your beloved Jesus, stripped, mocked, bruised, bloodied, and gasping for each breath in excruciating pain, fill your wearied mind, while your hands tremble from trauma and grief. Just the day before yesterday, you witnessed Jesus' agony unfold before you while standing motionless alongside Salome and Mary, James's mother, your arms intertwined in fear and mutual support. And as you watched Jesus die, you felt that any hope you'd ever had was dying as well.

Jesus had given you hope like none other, a hope that you had never before thought possible. You had first heard of Jesus when fantastic reports came to you of a wonderworking rabbi who was healing the sick throughout Galilee. The accounts sounded too remarkable to be true; rumors of miracle-workers often circulated throughout your world, and they inevitably turned out to be false. But the stories associated with Jesus were told with such sincerity and intensity that you decided to investigate for yourself. After all, for years you had struggled with illness and had prayed daily for a healing and relief that never came. Perhaps this Jesus might be legitimate after all, you thought; maybe God was in fact working through him, as certain of your neighbors asserted with great passion. At the very least, there was nothing to lose by seeking him out. And so one day, you did.

As soon as you laid eyes on Jesus, something in your gut assured you that he was no fraud. The authority in his voice, the tenderness in his eyes, and the gentleness of his touch as he rested his hands on your head were confirmation enough that he was a man of God, perhaps even a man *from* God. Those hands healed you of your illness, as your friends promised they would, and you decided, then and there, to assist Jesus in whatever way you were able. Along with other women, you supported him and the ministry of his disciples with your funds. Even more, you and this group actually joined company with the disciples. You traveled with Jesus, listened to him teach, asked him questions, witnessed him heal, and became his friends. It was rare enough that you were a woman whose finances were not controlled by a man, given the laws of the land and the prevailing culture. It was rarer still that you journeyed with Jesus' entourage; normally, women ventured from home only with the permission and presence of a male escort from her family. What was entirely unheard of, however, was that Jesus would welcome women into his group. Most Jewish rabbis—or teachers—would typically have an associated band of men who would accompany them and learn from their wisdom. Women, however, were never included—not even a rabbi's wife. Jesus had no wife, but he was surrounded by women like you. This raised quite a few eyebrows, especially among his many critics. Yet you counted it as one of your greatest joys.

Jesus was at ease around women, and he esteemed them highly. This was a comfort to you and a stark contrast to many men you had known. In addition to you, Jesus had other women friends, such as Mary and Martha, who were sisters. During his travels, Jesus readily engaged with women others would have shunned: a young woman caught in adultery; an older Samaritan woman, drawing water alone in the blazing noonday sun out of shame for her past life; and a long-suffering woman who had spent all her meager funds on doctors, seeking to heal a twelve-year flow of blood that made her "unclean" and therefore untouchable to observant Jews. Also, Jesus often illustrated his teaching with examples from the world of women, which he paralleled with examples from the world of men: mending garments and making wine, kneading leaven into dough and planting mustard seeds, and finding a lost coin from a wedding headdress and finding a lost sheep that had

wandered from a flock. He did this so that all his listeners could relate and understand because, without
exception, he loved all of them.

Widowed women were special objects of Jesus' compassion. Their loss of a husband too often meant the loss
of security, as they were placed at the mercy of their sons
or extended family. Those without family might be left
penniless and destitute, forced to beg in marketplaces or
on roadsides. Some, in fear and desperation, turned to
prostitution. When teaching once about the importance
of persistence in prayer, Jesus shared the example of a
widow who repeatedly nagged an indifferent judge until
she got what she needed. That, both he and you knew
well, is what widows were compelled to do when they
had no one to advocate for them or defend their rights.
On another occasion, Jesus praised the faith and gener-
osity of a widow who, in an act of love for God, placed
all she had—two small coins—into the treasury of the
Jerusalem Temple. In contrast, Jesus had nothing but dis-
dain for certain sanctimonious religious scribes who, to
line their coffers, would "devour widows' houses." On
one remarkable occasion, in the village of Nain, when
encountered with the heartbreaking funeral procession
for an only son, Jesus restored his widowed mother's
hope by returning him to life. And as you yourself witnessed, one of Jesus' last acts before he died was to provide for another widow soon to lose her only son: Mary,
his own mother. While hanging on a cross, he turned to
John, the solitary male disciple who hadn't fled in terror,
and placed Mary into his care as he said, "Behold, your
mother." Then, with a tenderness remarkable for one in
tremendous pain, he in turn gave John to Mary, saying,
"Behold, your son."

Jesus' mother had become very dear to you. You
shared both a name and a home region of Galilee: she
was from Nazareth, south and west of the Sea of Galilee, and you were from Magdala, on the sea's western

shore. Most importantly, you both shared a deep love for her son. While Jesus hung dying, she and John were closer to the foot of Jesus' cross while you and your companions stood at a distance. As the afternoon light waned under a darkened sky and the cicadas began to screech, you watched in frozen horror as Jesus cried out, hung his head, and breathed his last. Your chest tightened, and your heart seemed to stop as you witnessed Mary, overcome with grief, cradling her son's body after soldiers unceremoniously lowered him from the cross and yanked out the nails. And you followed behind as his body was taken to a rock tomb in a garden for a hasty burial before sundown, when the onset of the Jewish Sabbath prevented anything further being done. Joseph and Nicodemus, secret followers of Jesus who had arrived to claim the body, secured a large stone over the entrance of the tomb. Then they sent everyone away. Jesus was dead; it was over.

Or was it? As you alternately wept and paced last night and dreadful images from that day flooded your memory, recollections of things Jesus had said punctuated your grief. More than once, he had promised that while he would certainly be handed over by others to die, he would just as surely rise again from the dead on "the third day." This prediction had puzzled the disciples at the time, and they had puzzled you, too. Yet more than once, he had restored the dead to life: there was the son of the widow at Nain, for instance, and Lazarus, the brother of Mary and Martha. But how could he himself rise from the dead? You have no idea, but Jesus' words keep returning to you. As the night wears on and sunrise approaches, you realize that the third day is soon to arrive. Against what you think is your better judgment and in spite of your fatigue, you resolve to visit his tomb. You have no idea what you'll find there. Nevertheless, a faint glimmer of the hope you thought had died with Jesus begins to break through your inner gloom. And so you wrap your white shawl around your head, pull it tight for warmth, and head out into the chill darkness.

The full moon illuminates your steps as you make your way to the garden. You are afraid, but your love for Jesus and the thread of hope you cling to as a lifeline is greater than your fear. When you arrive, you fully expect the stone over the tomb's entrance to be firmly in place, just as you had last seen it. But to your astonishment, it has been rolled away. Unsure of what to do and fearful that perhaps Jesus' body has been stolen, you retrace your steps in haste and find John and another of Jesus' disciples, Peter. Alarmed, they accompany you back to the garden. As they approach, moonlight reveals the open grave, and they race to the entrance. Both step in, expecting to see Jesus' still and lifeless corpse wrapped in linen. The linen is there, neatly folded in a corner, but the body is nowhere to be seen. Without hesitation, the two men run back to inform their companions, leaving you alone. But you stand transfixed. The tears you thought had dried begin to flow again, accompanied by deep, heaving sobs.

Bending over, you peer into the tomb yourself. Instead of seeing Jesus' burial shroud, as the men had done, you see two angels in white. In unison, they ask why you are crying. "They have taken my Lord," you sputter, "and I don't know where they laid him." As you finish speaking these words, a twig snaps behind you. Startled, you turn and see a man you don't recognize, but he doesn't look threatening. In fact, he looks kind and, in a way, strangely familiar. Like the angels, he, too, asks why you are crying. When you ask for help in finding Jesus, he replies with one word: "Mary." He knows your name, and you know his voice. It is Jesus. You gasp in shock and rush to throw your arms around him. He smiles but does not permit a long embrace. "Stop holding on to me," he insisted, "for I have not yet ascended to the Father." Instead, he commissions you to tell his "brothers" that he has risen. You, a woman who had the courage to stay by Jesus at the cross and who in hope had ventured to his tomb in the darkness, are the first person to see him risen from the dead. And you are the one he has appointed to tell all the others. At this moment, you want nothing more than to remain with him and replace your tears of grief with tears of joy. Jesus, however, is firm: you must go forth and share the good news.

As the years have passed, the happiness of that day often springs to mind; your encounter with Jesus that morning is a memory you'll treasure forever. Nevertheless, you remain puzzled as to why Jesus had insisted that you not "hold on" to him. After all, you were dear friends: he loved you, and you loved him. So why couldn't you embrace him and extend the joy of that moment? And then, one day, you understand. You have encountered the risen Jesus once again—not in the damp chill outside a garden tomb but during the Lord's Supper, which Jesus' friends have been celebrating each week, and sometimes each day, ever since he ascended into heaven. Jesus had established this sacred meal the night before he died, when celebrating Passover with his disciples. During the meal's ritual, in a way you didn't fully understand, bread and wine changed into Jesus' body and blood. He himself became present in the assembly's midst. And when those gathered ate his body and drank his blood, in some mysterious way they were united with him, almost as if in an embrace.

This encounter with Jesus had been an occasion of joy; how could it not have been? Yet it was made clear that this encounter was not to be kept to one's self because, at the end of the meal, the entire assembly was sent forth to share it with the world, both in word and in deed. Like you on that beautiful resurrection morning, they had been given a commission to go and tell others of all they had seen and what they had heard. The risen

Jesus wasn't to be held on to; he was to be passed on instead. Once, he had sent you forth with a message and a ministry. Now, he sends everyone forth to be heralds of his hope, ambassadors of his mercy, and most of all, witnesses to his love.

Questions
for Journaling, Contemplation, or Conversation

1) What is your understanding of women's role in the Church? What do you think of this?

2) How comfortable do you feel sharing your faith, in either word or deed?

Stop and Pray

Risen Jesus,
You invite me to be your companion on life's journey so that you might heal me, teach me, walk by my side, and be my friend.
Empowered by the Eucharist, send me forth in courage to be a herald of your hope,
an ambassador of your mercy, and a witness to your love.
Amen.

Going Deeper

....

Mark 15:40–41	At the Crucifixion
Luke 8:2	Jesus Heals Mary Magdalene
Luke 8:1–2	Women Accompanying Jesus
Luke 8:3	Women Financially Support Jesus and the Disciples
Luke 10:38–42	Mary and Martha Are Friends of Jesus
Mark 5:25–34 John 4:4–26; 8:1–11	Jesus' Interactions with Women
Luke 5:36–37; 13:18–21; 15:1–10	Women's Imagery in Jesus' Teaching
Mark 12:38–44 Luke 7:11–17; 18:1–8 John 19:26–27	Jesus' Compassion for Widows
Matthew 27:57–61 John 19:38–42	Mary Magdalene Witnesses Jesus' Burial
Luke 9:22; 18:31–34	Jesus Promises to Rise on the Third Day
Luke 7:11–17 John 11:1–44	The Dead Restored to Life by Jesus
John 20:1–10	Empty Tomb Discovered by Mary Magdalene
John 20:11–18	Mary Magdalene Encounters the Risen Jesus

14. JOHN

SACRIFICE

Who was St. John?

St. John and his older brother, James, grew up fishing in the Sea of Galilee, as had their father, Zebedee. Until Jesus called them to be apostles, James and John had followed John the Baptist. Jesus would nickname them "Sons of Thunder" and, along with Peter, allow them to accompany him for significant occasions: his raising a young girl from the dead, his transfiguration when Moses and Elijah appeared alongside him, and his praying in agony shortly before his arrest. John remained with Jesus at his crucifixion, when Jesus entrusted his mother into John's care with the words, "Behold, your mother." Tradition associates John with the "beloved disciple" in the gospel which bears John's name and asserts that he was the only apostle not to die a martyr's death.

• • • • • •

You aren't going to run away. Not today, at least. Just last night, you had fled into the darkness after Jesus was arrested. All the other disciples had done so as well—except Judas, the betrayer, who with a kiss had singled out Jesus to the soldiers he'd led there. Although torchlight and moonglow had been the only illumination, the shadows couldn't mask the fear on Judas's face. He was scared, like you. But you were in danger, and he was not. Your heart had been racing, and your mind was racing, too: Should you fight, or should you flee? But when Jesus himself refused to fight and surrendered to his captors, terror and a basic desire for self-preservation overwhelmed all else in your spinning head, and you sprinted from the scene.

No one had chased you, and for a brief moment, you felt grateful to be safe. But once you had caught your breath, you found yourself alone, outside, cold, and still scared and confused. For the remainder of that seemingly endless night, you huddled in darkness, watching the moon creep silently through the heavens. And as night slowly surrendered to dawn, your primal fear gave way to shame and grief. Now guilt grips your heart; you had abandoned the side of one who had once called you to his side and kept you there for some of the most significant moments of his life. Along with Peter and your brother James, Jesus had allowed you to witness things that your fellow disciples had not. At Capernaum, Jesus had permitted only the three of you to watch him heal the daughter of Jairus, a synagogue official, while a skeptical crowd waited outside. It was again just the three of you who stood with Jesus on a mountaintop, quaking in awe and fear, as he was transfigured in white before you, the voice of God proclaimed him to be his Son, and the ancient prophets Moses and Elijah appeared beside him. And then, only hours ago, in the dark of a dreadful night, Jesus had asked you, your brother, and Peter to remain with him as he prayed, in evident agony at a garden just outside Jerusalem's city walls.

You understood now that Jesus knew his arrest was imminent; that's why he wanted you with him. Yet you had failed him at what was surely the most painful moment of his life. First, you and your companions had fallen asleep while he longed for your companionship; then, you had fled the scene, leaving him to face his captors alone. You hadn't betrayed him like Judas, but you had failed him, which in your mind was almost as bad. Having abandoned Jesus left you with nothing but pain, and you couldn't undo what you had done. But you could return to him, which you had resolved to do at morning light. When the sun finally rose, its warming rays instilled in you some much-needed courage, and you set forth in spite of any risk to yourself. Your love for Jesus had cast out your fear.

He isn't hard to find. The city is buzzing about his arrest, even at such an early hour. Keeping a discreet distance, you follow the crowds winding their way through the narrow streets until you arrive at the *praetorium* of Pilate, the Roman prefect. Jesus has been imprisoned there overnight in anticipation of his trial. Shortly after the proceedings begin, Pilate appears atop a high staircase, where he presents Jesus to the assembled onlookers. While those around you jeer and demand his crucifixion, you are again overwhelmed by grief. When he is publicly whipped and soaked in blood, you stand frozen in horror. But by the time he is forced to carry the crossbeam of his cross to his execution site, you feel numb, as if your emotions have shut down altogether. Never before have you witnessed such cruelty to another human being; never before have you seen one you loved suffer so much pain.

After you follow Jesus and his armed guard of four soldiers outside the city, a trio of upright posts secured in limestone comes into view, and you know that you have arrived at the place where Jesus is to die. You scan the crowd, looking for a familiar face. None of the other disciples are there. You are disappointed but not surprised. At supper last night, Jesus had insisted to you and your companions that your faith would be shaken and that he would be abandoned. "I will strike the

shepherd," Jesus quoted from scripture, "and the sheep
of the flock will be dispersed." He had been right, you
think, just as he always was. But then, practically hidden
under their veils, you see faces you do recognize: those
of Mary, Jesus' mother; Mary from Magdala, a close follower of Jesus like you; and yet another Mary, the wife
of Clopas, who is also a follower. Jesus' mother's eyes
meet yours, but neither of you speak as you are both
sorrowful beyond words. Instead, you walk over to the
three women, stand behind then in solidarity, and watch
Jesus be nailed to his cross. Seeing him suffer, you feel
devastated and helpless. But you aren't going to run
away; you no longer feel afraid.

As it is, there is nothing to be afraid of. Yes, facing
you are armed Roman soldiers who have no love for
Jews like yourself. But now that Jesus hangs dying, they
are unconcerned about the presence of a solitary male
disciple. You are no threat to them, and they seem more
interested in casting lots to see who will keep Jesus'
clothing and then take it back to the safety of their bar-
racks. Their primary duty now is to prevent you or anyone else from trying to rescue Jesus and ensure that he
dies before sundown. And they are successful. Yet before
he dies, the soldiers do something remarkable. Jesus
has just whispered, "I thirst," after raising his head in
obvious pain. One soldier places a sponge on a sprig of
hyssop, soaks it with wine, and raises it to Jesus' lips. It
is a small gesture of human compassion near the end of
a most inhuman act. After taking a sip, Jesus declares,
"It is finished," bows his head, and breathes his last.

Tears stream down your cheeks as the women with
you weep openly as well. But your sorrow is oddly
mixed with a sense of disappointment. You wonder:
Were "It is finished" really Jesus' final words? They seem
like a whimpering anticlimax to a life lived with such
power and authority. During his hours on the cross,
Jesus had spoken very little. That was understandable,

given that he was gasping for breath and in tremendous pain. At one point, Jesus mustered up the strength to place his mother into your care, an example of the love that characterized everything he did. That was a noble gesture, and you had expected his final words to be noble as well. Something wise, meaningful, profound, significant. But no; all he could manage was "It is finished."

Just days before, Jesus had spoken of "glory." The hour had come for him to glorify the Father, he explained, which he would accomplish by being "lifted up." Yet you had just seen him "lifted up," and there was nothing glorious about it at all. There had been a sign above him, proclaiming him to be a king, and a cruel crown of thorns had been forced onto his head. But these didn't honor his nobility; they mocked it. A heavenly host should have surrounded him, but he had been flanked by two criminals. His being lifted up had been humiliating, not glorious. Perhaps, stripped bare, bloodied, naked, and abandoned, he'd been aware of that. Maybe "It is finished" meant "I am finished." In other words, "I've been defeated."

Thinking that Jesus had died a failure breaks your heart. And as your heart breaks, you look on in resignation as the soldiers proceed to break the legs of the men crucified alongside Jesus. This is common practice, you know, intended to suffocate a condemned person by preventing him from lifting his body and filling his lungs. But when they go to break Jesus' legs, they discover that he is already dead. One thrusts a lance into his side instead, just in case there is a trace of life still in him. It is a tragic conclusion to a magnificent life.

The finality of what has just happened begins to sink in. Your head swirls with conflicting thoughts and emotions. Nevertheless, one seemingly random question persistently keeps coming to mind: Is it significant that Jesus' legs hadn't been broken? Given that your beloved Jesus has just died, you are angry that such a trivial matter keeps intruding on your thoughts. But then you recall something from the night before. For you and every Jew, it was always the most special night of the year: Passover, the ancient Jewish commemoration of God's having freed your ancestors, the Israelites, from slavery in Egypt. The celebration was centered upon a meal in which a lamb, sacrificed that day in the great Jerusalem Temple, was eaten amidst ancient prayers and traditions. The lamb had to be perfect, without blemish, to be suitable for sacrifice to God. Anything less would be an insult, a sacrilege. Specifically, you recalled, the scriptures mandated that sacrificed lambs could have no broken bones. Just like Jesus had no broken bones. In a moment of insight, you recall that when the high priest at the Temple sacrificed the last of thousands of lambs on Passover day, he ceremoniously announced, "It is finished!" The same as Jesus' final words. His crucifixion hadn't been a defeat after all; instead, it had been the perfect sacrifice of a lamb. You had heard others refer to Jesus as the "Lamb of God." Now you understand what that meant.

Jesus was a sacrificial lamb—a Passover lamb—and somehow this sacrifice has glorified the Father. That answers the question of why his legs had not been broken. But this gives rise to another question in your mind. "It is finished" was the declaration of a high priest who offered sacrifice as well as the final words of Jesus, who had been offered in sacrifice. But where was the priest in Jesus' sacrifice? Was it the Temple high priest, who would have slaughtered his final lamb just as Jesus died? Or was it Pilate, who consented to his crucifixion? Perhaps it was the soldier who nailed him to his cross, or maybe the one who lanced his side? But none of these possibilities make any sense. There can be only one conclusion: Jesus had been both priest and victim in his sacrifice. No one had offered him up; he had offered up himself. Jesus had even spoken of this once. His words hadn't made sense at the time, but now their meaning becomes clear. "I lay down my life in order to take it up again," Jesus had explained. "No one takes it from me, but I lay it down on my own."

Still, in spite of this new perspective into the nature of Jesus' death, your grief remains. As you watch his lifeless body laid in a nearby tomb and continue to reflect on his final words, you conclude that many things are now indeed finished: your hopes, your dreams, your ministry, his ministry, his sacrifice as the Lamb of God. Passover lambs are meant to die, after all. God had commanded that long ago. But then again, you realize with a sudden start, that's not all God had commanded. Passover lambs were also meant to be eaten; a meal was necessary to complete the sacrifice. Until now, Passover lambs had been consumed at Passover suppers. But how and where was Jesus to be eaten, if that were even possible? For this, Jesus had issued a new commandment, given to you and your fellow disciples at your Passover supper with him last night: "Take and eat; this is my body."

Your grief has now partially lifted; a small measure of hope now tempers your sadness. Three days later, your grief is lifted completely when you encounter Jesus alive, having risen from the dead. He's laid down his life, as he promised, only to take it up again. The one you'd abandoned but returned to has now returned to you, never to die again. As both priest and victim, his sacrifice was "finished"; there was no longer any need for thousands of lambs to be slaughtered year after year as had always been done. And as the lamb-once-slain, Jesus himself would be consumed by those who love him as blessed bread and wine. The Passover supper has been replaced by what has come to be called the Lord's Supper, which would become one of your greatest joys. "Christ our Passover has been sacrificed for us!" you would often exclaim with your friends. "Therefore, let us keep the feast!"

Questions
for Journaling, Contemplation, or Conversation

1) Has fear ever compromised your love for another or for God? Has love ever conquered your fear?

2) What is your understanding of the glory of God? Does the crucifixion factor into it?

Stop and Pray

Lamb of God,
At times my belief in you calls me to do that which is difficult,
humiliating, painful, and frightening.
Fill me with love to cast out my fear, that I may remain steadfast in faith,
imitate your sacrifice, and keep your Eucharistic feast in joy.
Amen.

Going Deeper

Mark 14:43–50	Disciples Flee at Jesus' Arrest
Mark 5:21–24, 35–43	The Healing of Jairus's Daughter
Mark 9:2–8	Transfiguration of Jesus
Mark 9:32–42	Jesus in Gethsemane
Mark 15:1–19	Trial and Mockery of Jesus
Mark 14:27	Disciples' Fear Foretold
John 19:25	At the Foot of the Cross

John 19:23–24	Soldiers Cast Lots for Jesus' Clothing
John 19:25	At the Foot of the Cross
John 19:28–30	Wine Offered to Jesus Before He Dies
John 19:26–27	Jesus Places His Mother into John's Care
John 12:27–36	Jesus Will Glorify the Father
John 19:1–3, 19	Nobility of Jesus Mocked
Mark 15:27	Two Criminals Crucified with Jesus
John 19:31–34	Legs of Jesus Remain Unbroken
Exodus 12	Origin of Hebrew Passover Rituals
Exodus 12:46	Passover Lambs Could Have No Broken Bones
John 1:35	Jesus Called "The Lamb of God"
John 10:17–18	Jesus to Lay Down and Take Up His Life
Matthew 26:26	Disciples Instructed to Eat Jesus' Body
John 20:19–20	The Risen Jesus Meets His Disciples
1 Corinthians 5:7	Followers Exhorted to Keep the Feast of Jesus

R. Scott Hurd is a Catholic speaker and award-winning author who has more than twenty years' experience in professional ministry. He serves as senior director for leadership formation with Catholic Charities USA.

Hurd is the author of five books, including *Forgiveness: A Catholic Approach,* which received an Excellence in Publishing award from the Association of Catholic Publishers. *When Faith Feels Fragile: Hope for the Wary, Weak, and Wandering* earned a second-place award in 2014 from the Catholic Press Association and was also a finalist in the ACP Excellence in Publishing awards. Hurd also is the author of two books in *The Living Gospel* seasonal series from Ave Maria Press.

Hurd graduated from the University of Richmond (cum laude) in 1989 with a degree in accounting and business administration. He received his bachelor of theology degree from Oxford University (UK) in 1993. He lives in his hometown of Alexandria, Virginia, with his three children.

AVE

AVE MARIA PRESS

Founded in 1865, Ave Maria Press,
a ministry of the Congregation of
Holy Cross, is a Catholic publishing
company that serves the spiritual and
formative needs of the Church and its
schools, institutions, and ministers;
Christian individuals and families; and
others seeking spiritual nourishment.

For a complete listing of titles from

Ave Maria Press

Sorin Books

Forest of Peace

Christian Classics

visit www.avemariapress.com

AVE MARIA PRESS
Notre Dame, IN
A Ministry of the United States Province of Holy Cross